Praise for

POTENT
LEADERSHIP

In a very noisy world of influencers and self-serving "leaders," Ruby offers a refreshing and much-needed take on what it truly means to lead and step into our fullest power and expression. *Potent Leadership* offers an insightful and confronting look in the mirror for all of us to deepen into our truth, challenge the status quo, and call us forward into our highest levels of integrity. This is a must-read for anyone looking to awaken to their fullest potential and start living the life they were meant to live.

—**ALEXI PANOS**, Master Embodiment Coach & Trainer, Cofounder of
The Bridge Method and Elementum Coaching Institute, Author of
50 Ways to Yay! and *Now or Never*, and Cofounder of the nonprofit
E.P.I.C. (Everyday People Initiating Change) and The Sister Society

Every coach, entrepreneur, and ambitious human needs to own a copy of this book. Ruby breaks down leadership in an articulate and practical way that doesn't lose its potency.

Potent Leadership is a well-written handbook on how to be a strong leader and really make an impact. It will encourage you to rethink your messaging and double down on authenticity. And in doing so, you will call in new clients and opportunities. This is for real leaders, wanting to make a real impact.

—**AREN BAHIA**, Entrepreneur, Speaker, Coach, Cofounder of YogiLab,
Founder of Karma House Bali, Conscious Arts Tattoos, and Full Reset Coaching

In a world full of influencers and imposters, Ruby Fremon stands authentically in her power, gripping a life-sized mirror, revealing the depths of what we often choose not to see, so we can truly begin to heal. *Potent Leadership* is the book the social landscape doesn't want, but desperately needs. So, remove your false sense of identity, open your heart, and be ready to dive through a portal of benevolent leadership awakening.

—**DR. BRETT JONES**, Author of *Know Who the F*ck You Are*,
CEO of The Source Chiropractic, Creator of Kairos Training Culture,
Sacred MC, DJ Meta, Healing Facilitator, Husband, Father, Human

We are in uncertain times, and the world needs strength, truth, and compassion. Ruby has clearly articulated not only how to understand what this means but also how you can embody this.

I have read word-for-word Ruby's well-written masterpiece *Potent Leadership*, and I must say, I am finding myself challenging my own inner parameters and standards of what it means to be a true leader.

Pick this book up and challenge yourself to integrate these potent lessons of wisdom from Ruby Fremon.

—**JOEL BROWN**, Master Coach and Speaker and Founder of Addicted2Success

Sooner or later every human being will come to terms with two very important facts. One, they are here to do far greater things than the external validation provides, and two, it all starts with having a very healthy relationship with who they really are and not what they want the world to approve of. Ruby tackles all of this and more in *Potent Leadership*, giving the reader permission to explore their entire being and lead from their highest truth.

—**MATT GOTTESMAN**, Entrepreneur, Founder, Writer, Podcaster
& Host of the Hustle Sold Separately, Multidisciplinary

In a day and age of fake, *Potent Leadership* is the reality check this world needs. It is a practical guide that invites leaders to stand in their power, own their gifts, and relentlessly lead from their hearts. Through beautiful story-telling and deep empirical research, Ruby takes the reader on a journey to unlock and express their most authentic self. *Potent Leadership* is the new gold standard for leadership books and is a must-read for anyone looking to become a more impactful and inspiring leader.

—**BRANDEN COLLINSWORTH**, Entrepreneur, Nike Master Trainer &
Yoga Teacher, Founder of Warrior Retreats, Founding Expert of Mine'd

RUBY FREMON

POTENT LEADERSHIP

DROP THE MASK,
IGNITE THE REAL YOU,
AND RECLAIM THE LEADER WITHIN.

Hardcover ISBN: 9781737133803
eBook ISBN: 9781737133810

BUS071000 BUSINESS & ECONOMICS / Leadership
SEL027000 SELF-HELP / Personal Growth / Success

Cover design by Kevin Fremon
Edited by Melissa Miller
Typeset by Kaitlin Barwick

www.rubyfremon.com

This book is dedicated to you, the leader who
is ready to stand with conviction in who you BE.

No more holding back, no more performing, and no more masks.

You're ready to be free, and this book is here to support
you on that journey. It's time to reclaim your potency.

Contents

PART 1:
FAKE AF

PART 2:
WHO YOU BE

PART 3:
POTENCY

ACKNOWLEDGMENTS

I would love to say that I always knew I wanted to write a book, but that's just not the truth. Up until my early thirties, I honestly believed that I wasn't worthy of anything good and that my voice and presence didn't matter. It wasn't until I devoted myself to my journey that I started to realize what I had to say mattered, and that my life mattered. My journey of reclaiming my potency helped me understand the value that I have to offer myself and the people around me.

The year 2012 is when this journey began. That's also when I started sharing more of me with the online world. At first, I was timid and wore a lot of masks, but I was determined to share my story because I thought if I could help one person feel less alone with what they were going through, that was enough. That was also the year that my husband, Kevin, came into my life.

We met on Twitter. Yes, Twitter. I had just ended an abusive, four-and-a-half-year relationship and was in the depth of my addiction. It was my most pivotal rock-bottom moment, but it was also the beginning of my awakening. I was desperate to get my life back and feel worthy, which is why the first leg of my journey was self-love. I needed to learn how to love myself because, up until that point, I never did.

I ended up creating a list of declarations—kind of like a vision board, but with statements. And one of those declarations was "I will be living and working in Los Angeles by the end of 2013." It was March 2012 at the time, and I was living in my hometown of Vancouver, BC. My initial thought was that I'd find a job at a tech startup, get a visa, and move to LA. But that wasn't the case . . .

I started stalking multiple tech startups, looking for social media positions because, at the time, I was a social media manager and strategist. That's when Instacanvas popped into my radar—a tech startup that made canvas prints from Instagram images. The company looked cool, and they had just started receiving media attention, so I decided to go after them like the clever social media manager that I was . . . by stalking their social feeds, connecting with their founders, and establishing a relationship.

I noticed that they had launched a "Twitter Tuesday" contest, so I thought that this would be a great way to get their attention. The contest asked participants to tweet Instagram images that they would want to print on canvas from their website. I entered, selecting an image with a quote that said, "Gratitude is the open door to abundance." And to my surprise, I won! One of their cofounders, Kevin Fremon, tweeted me to let me know, asking me to send him an email. What I didn't know at the time was that he had handpicked me from the entries based on my avatar.

I sent Kevin an email, and his reply was a little flirtatious. What you need to understand is that, at that time, I had just hit rock bottom and my self-worth was shattered. Not only was I not looking to date, but I sure as hell did not feel worthy of dating a handsome cofounder of a successful tech startup in LA. However, with that being said, there was something about him—something familiar. Our email exchange quickly moved to text messages, a phone call, and within a week, a Skype call. That's when everything changed.

There he was . . . the face I had seen in dreams my entire life. The familiarity was uncanny and kind of freaked me out, but it was like my heart just knew. He felt the same way about me. Unfortunately, timing was not the best for either of us, as he had just started dating someone and I was a mess. So we went our separate ways.

Over the next eight months, I went on a roller coaster ride with my addiction. On one hand, I was doing great! I was eating much healthier, working out regularly, reading books on spirituality, and attending personal development events. But on the other hand, I was still partying, doing drugs and drinking, unaware of the depth of my addiction. It wasn't until I experienced a major concussion in December 2012 that things changed.

I was high at a nightclub, and I fainted headfirst into the concrete floor. My entire body felt like it had shattered to a million pieces, and when I finally came to, I refused to go to the hospital because I held so much shame around my addiction. I went home and, when the concussion stretched on for more than a few days, I took myself to the hospital, where I was diagnosed with post-concussion syndrome.

My symptoms were unbearable. I suffered from persistent migraines, extreme sensitivity to light and sound, horrible pain in my head, neck and upper back, brain fog and confusion that made it hard for me to string words together, and depression so deep that I struggled to speak without bursting out into tears. Eventually, the doctors found nerve damage in my brain and placed me on medication in January 2013.

Within twelve days of taking the medication, the fog began to lift. But that's not all . . . I also started to feel clearer on what I wanted. It was as if my brain had totally rewired. The old, self-sabotaging version of myself was dead, and a new me was emerging. I knew what I didn't want, but I was unclear on what I wanted. At that point, I still wasn't sure what I was worthy of having or experiencing. So I decided that the best way to change my life would be to do the exact opposite of what I would normally do. That's the exact week when Kevin sent me a text message that said, "Should we give this a go?"

Now the old me would have said, "Fuck no," because she didn't feel worthy. But this new tactic for changing my life had me saying something different. I said yes, and things moved quickly after that.

Within a month, we said, "I love you," over text, and we finally met in person a month after when he came up to Canada to visit me. Two months later, he proposed, and we got married in LA in January 2014. Remember that declaration I told you about? "I will be living and working in Los Angeles by the end of 2013." Well . . . it came true. I just never thought it would happen by marrying my soulmate.

I share all of this with you because without Kevin, none of this would be possible. He even designed this book cover! I truly believe that Kevin came into my life when he did to show me what could be possible. He was the first person to have ever seen me—really SEE me. He was the first person to hear me, acknowledge me, and love me for who I was, without my masks.

Kevin, thank you so much for your unwavering support. Thank you for loving me through all the ups and downs and for being my anchor. This book would not have happened without you, because your presence in my life is the reason that I have felt so safe to be me, in my potency. No one else sees me the way you do, and that's such a gift. I am so grateful that the universe conspired for us to meet in this lifetime. I love you to the moon and back.

Throughout this book, you'll also hear stories about my upbringing and my parents. What I want you to understand is that, today, I have an incredible relationship with my parents and oldest brother. In my journey, I realized something that changed my perspective, and it's that everyone is always doing their absolute best with what they know, what they've experienced, and what's available to them. With that being said, my parents did their absolute best to raise me. They raised me the only way they knew how, and that was through their own life experiences. We've had our share of ups and downs, but we are closer than ever today, and I have a deeper appreciation for who they are.

Mom and Dad, thank you for raising me the way that you did. Thank you for loving me in your own ways and for showing me the true meaning of family. I truly wouldn't be who I am without you. I love you, and I am proud to be your daughter.

To Bob, my oldest brother, thank you for always being my protector and for always having my back. Thank you for scaring away the bullies at school and for taking a stand for me when no one else in our family did. I love you.

And to Rocky, my middle brother, thank you for playing a pivotal role in one of my greatest life lessons. I'll always love you, no matter what.

Writing this book was a journey within itself. I can't even begin to tell you how many tears I shed, how much frustration I felt, and how many times I rewrote chapters. To be fair, writing a book on leadership, in 2020, was a feat within itself—that was a year when our entire world changed and the veils for leadership were lifted. I am so grateful to have had my writing coach, Azul Terronez, by my side throughout the process. Not only did he make me ditch my original book idea, but he also helped me uncover the real message that I wanted and needed to share, which became this book.

Azul, thank you for your patience, encouragement, and calming presence as I navigated the tornado of emotions throughout this book-writing process. You are a master at what you do.

A huge part of my journey has been with the support of plant medicine (more on this in later chapters). Ayahuasca (otherwise known as "grandmother medicine") has helped me break down my walls and face the traumas from this lifetime and the lineages before me. She's helped me heal in more ways than I can describe. Thank you, Mama Aya, for helping me see what needed to be healed. Thank you to my maestro in Peru, Papa Gilberto Mahua, my plant medicine facilitators, Robin and Alicia, and to my plant medicine family (you know who you are). I am forever humbled by the work that we've done together and continue to do.

And to you, my beloved community. This entire journey has been unfolding before your eyes as I've been transparently sharing online since the beginning. Some of you have been there since the start, and others have found your way to me throughout my journey, but there's one thing you all have in common, and that's your incredible hearts. There are so many times when your words have lifted me up—whether it's through an email, a DM, a text message, or a comment on social media. You have been there for me, and I am so grateful for your presence in my life. Thank you for your continued love and support.

Finally, to the constant presence in my life. God, Spirit, Pachamama . . .

Thank you.

Thank you.

Thank you.

A'ho.

INTRODUCTION

"But what makes you unique?"

I don't know about you, but when I was just starting my coaching business, I'd get asked this question all the time, and it frustrated the shit out of me. Whether it was a business coach asking me to identify my USP (unique selling proposition) or another mentor asking me to identify what makes me different from the rest of the life coaches, I always stumbled to land on something. Back then, I was rocking my long pink hair, so I found myself defaulting to "I'm the life coach with pink hair and tattoos." But soon, pink hair became a trend, and I found myself back in a space of frustration, struggling to identify why people would want to work with me.

No matter how it's worded, whether it's "What makes you unique?" or "What makes you different?" or "What's your USP?", these types of questions are all ways of asking "What makes you so special that people would choose you?"

It's a question that challenges your self-worth, and yet the wording often requires you to find an answer that lies outside of who you are.

For example: "What makes me different is my ABC framework, which helps entrepreneurs create $10K months in just ten days!"

You need to understand that any external solutions you provide lead you astray from your potency. You will continue to struggle to identify what makes you unique if you focus on finding those answers outside of yourself. What makes you unique isn't a framework, process, or system. Nor is it the color of your hair, your tattoos, your cool glasses, or the fact that you say "fuck" a lot.

What makes you unique is the totality of all that you are.

Your values, your gifts, your voice, your presence, your energy, your personality, your physical self, your tonality, your essence, your skills, your attributes, your service, your wisdom, your experience, your story . . . ALL this combined is what makes you unique. This is why looking outside of yourself won't help you find what makes you different, and creating an external solution won't really differentiate you from others—the real answer is **who you be.**

There are far too many leaders focused on external tactics to draw people into their movements. If you really want to stand out, you have to show up as the fullest expression of who you be. And this starts with you cultivating a deep understanding of who you be.

What makes you YOU is not what you have or what you have to offer. It's who you BE.

I describe "potency" as the medicine that you have to offer when you are being the fullest expression of who you be.

It's who you are when you turn the dial all the way up and give yourself the freedom to be all that makes you you—without fear of judgment. Being your potent self is being who you are when no one's watching or listening—it's about unapologetically expressing those parts of yourself that you've been most fearful of expressing, due to how you've been made to feel about yourself. Your potency is a gift—it's the medicine that you need and it's the medicine that the world needs. We all have this medicine within us, but most of us have never been taught how to share this medicine with the world. In fact, you've most likely been trained to do the opposite . . .

To play small, to hide, to sacrifice, to conform, to obey, to comply, to meet the expectations of others, to cower to the pressures of society, to be like "them," to fit in, to bite your tongue, to hold back on sharing your truth. All of this dilutes your potency, leaving you as a watered-down version of yourself.

I know this all too well. Living with the pressures of being an Indian woman, training to be the "perfect" Indian wife or daughter-in-law, being shut down or shunned anytime I questioned my parents, being told over and over and over again that I'm too moody, and having to fit a cultural expectation of how I look and how I show up . . . all of which led me down a path that wasn't my own.

To offer you a deeper perspective and understanding, I think it's important to share with you the story that got me here.

I got married at twenty years old and thought I knew what I wanted. But the truth is, I wanted what my parents wanted for me, just so that I could receive their love and approval.

It was at that age that I also experienced the deepest trauma in my life—the disconnection with my middle brother. I have two older brothers, and growing up, I was closest to my middle brother. I saw him as my friend, my confidant, and my protector; I had placed him on a pedestal. Things were said that caused a ripple of disconnection within our family, starting with me. I was painted as the black sheep of the family, accused of things that I never did or said, and I found myself apologizing over and over again, just to make things better. But things never got better—they got worse. And within a couple of years, I witnessed most of my family turn their backs on me, including my parents. I felt unsupported, unloved, unseen, and unacknowledged for what I was experiencing. But most of all, I felt deeply misunderstood.

At the age of twenty-two, my depression hit a breaking point. I could barely get out of bed because I was experiencing tremendous pain in my body. I saw a few doctors and specialists and was eventually diagnosed with clinical depression, fibromyalgia, rheumatoid arthritis, and anxiety disorder. They put me on a cocktail of prescriptions—five total, one of which was a benzodiazepine commonly known as Ativan.

I quickly became an addict. After feeling so much for so long, it felt good to not feel, and Ativan helped me do just that. No one questioned why I was getting my prescription refilled more often than was recommended, so I kept refilling the bottle. By this point, my marriage was a mess, as was I. The life I was living didn't feel like the life that I wanted, and I ended up there because of my people-pleasing ways.

I followed *their* rules, I lived my life to fulfill *their* expectations, I obeyed, I conformed, and I sacrificed my potency all in an attempt to feel loved and accepted . . . and I felt none of that. In fact, I felt so unloved that it led me to believe that life wasn't worth living.

At the age of twenty-three, I attempted suicide by swallowing an entire bottle of Ativan with a bottle of rum. I had reached a point in my life where nothing felt good. I felt unloved, unseen, unacknowledged, and misunderstood. I was done. But life wasn't done with me.

I had passed out and a couple of hours later, I was shaken awake by my husband. The first thought that passed in my mind was "Shit, this didn't work." And that's when I saw the look of disappointment in his eyes, again, leaving me to feel as if I wasn't good enough.

I was forced to detox. Within a week, I realized that I was given another chance, and I wanted more than anything to use it. At this point, I felt disillusioned by the medical industry because they paved this path of addiction for me, so I decided to seek out holistic support. That's when I discovered naturopathic care. At the age of twenty-three, I started my lifelong health journey.

My naturopath weened me off all my prescriptions, placed me on a healthier eating regime, and slowly but surely, I started to feel amazing. I felt better than I had ever felt before. I started working out regularly (taking care of my health) and began to gain more clarity on my needs. Improving my health helped me see things differently because, for the first time in my life, I was prioritizing myself. And that's when things started to shift in my marriage.

I married a man who I loved, but as the years went by and I started to honor my well-being, I started to notice just how different we were. I still had yet to really know who I was and uncover my potency, but I started to understand who I wasn't, and that was enough for me to know that this relationship wasn't the right relationship for me. He was everything I thought I wanted, but looking back, he was everything my parents wanted for me. After multiple marriage counseling sessions, it was clear to me that this wasn't going to work. But how could I, an Indian woman, leave my husband? Divorce is frowned upon in our culture, and my parents were already feeling so disappointed in me due to the situation with my middle brother. I didn't have the courage to just leave, so I cowered and did something that I thought I'd never do . . . I cheated. I felt like this would be easier than to admit that I just wasn't happy, because speaking my truth still felt so foreign to me.

We ended the marriage, and I carried the shame of the infidelity with me for years. The divorce cast a definite shadow on me within our cultural society, and my parents did not approve, but for the first time in my life, at the age of twenty-six, I felt free. What I didn't know at that time was that this feeling of freedom was external, not internal. As such, it was a temporary sense of freedom.

I lived on my own for the first time in my life and began partying a lot. I was trying to catch up for lost time, but that led me into a world of drugs and alcohol. Despite my attempt to be healthier, I was still harboring so much pain and trauma that I had yet to address. I found myself back in my people-pleasing ways, conforming to the ideals of society, masking my truth in exchange to be liked, loved, and accepted.

I diluted my potency so much that by the time I was thirty years old, I was just a shell of who I was, living my life to please others while numbing the pain of my diluted potency with drugs and alcohol.

Living your life with diluted potency is like living a slow death. You run on autopilot, killing your self-worth, being completely detached from your truth, your voice, and your essence. You're a shape-shifter, constantly reshaping yourself to please or conform to those around you while dismissing anything that makes you you. Leading your purpose with diluted potency is very much the same because you're constantly questioning yourself, doubting yourself, feeling unworthy, and showing up to "fit in" or be "liked," pushing away those you're truly here to serve.

And yet you do this all the time because you've been trained to.

Your potency acts as autofiltration, pushing away those who aren't aligned while attracting those who are. If you've been wondering why you're not attracting the right clients, friendships, partnerships, relationships, experiences, or opportunities . . . this is why.

Have you ever scrolled through your social media feed only to feel like every single leader is saying the same thing, using the same filters, and doing the same shit? Or attended an event where all the leaders speaking on stage are delivering similar performances that lack real depth? This is the result of living in a society that encourages us to dilute our potency so we can fit in and be accepted.

But you're not here to fit in. Nor are you here to gain the acceptance of others.

You're here to lead your purpose, and your purpose can only be led by you. This means you must boil down that diluted medicine within you until it becomes potent. You must put an end to playing small, to hiding, to sacrificing, to conforming, to obeying, to complying, to meeting the expectations of others, to cowering to the pressures of society, to be like "them," to fit in, to bite your tongue, to hold back on sharing your truth. And you must practice this over and over and over again until it becomes your default behavior.

You owe it to yourself to live your life as you.

I hit rock bottom in 2012, and this served as the greatest awakening in my life. This was the awakening that led me to my soul mate, husband, and biggest source of support, Kevin—the first person in my life who has left me feeling deeply seen, heard, acknowledged, and understood. It was also the awakening that led me to my true purpose because this was when I started my journey of uncovering my potency. I'll share more on this rock bottom moment later in the book, but right now, I want to emphasize that you can unleash your potency at any time. Refuse to let your past dictate your future, and instead, let yourself be led by the possibility of creating something better for yourself by uncovering who you are (or as I prefer saying, who you be).

Your potency is the greatest medicine that you have to offer the world and yourself. It's what makes you unique and different and will help you stand out from other leaders. It's what will attract those you're truly meant to serve because it gives them an opportunity to really see you. And you will become your most potent self when you lead your life as the fullest expression of who you be.

I wrote this book to support you in reclaiming your potency, and I did so because I understand the depth of pain that comes with living your life as a diluted version of who you are. But this book won't do the work for you—that's up to you. This book is simply a guide to support you on your journey to becoming a Potent Leader.

In part 1, we dissect all the ways in which you aren't showing up as a Potent Leader. You need to understand what a Potent Leader is NOT before moving on to part 2. In part 2, you will dive deep to uncover the experiences that have influenced who you are being today. This work is crucial. In my experience (both personally and in working with hundreds of leaders around the world), I found that the better we understand WHY we're being who we're being, the easier it becomes to break free from our false identities to become our potent selves. So as repetitive as things may feel at times, it's necessary to ensure that you truly understand who you are. And finally, in part 3, you'll begin to put into practice everything you've learned, to be the fullest expression of who you are, and to show up as the Potent Leader you know you're here to be.

But be warned . . . this book may trigger you. You may feel called out at times—and that's a good thing. I encourage you to lean into your triggers, and instead of reacting to them, observe yourself in a triggered state. Your triggers are your biggest teachers because underneath that trigger is where you'll find your traumas, your wounds, and your pain. Work through the resistance you may feel and know that I am here with you.

Your potency is there, beneath all the protective mechanisms and false identities that you've built. And together, we will unleash that potency.

PART 1:

FAKE AF

CHAPTER 1:
SELF-CONSCIOUS LEADERSHIP

The online space is noisy AF with leaders claiming to be THE answer, and to know all the answers. And you're contributing to that noise by enlisting yourself in the race to become known as an expert and go-to person in your industry, because this is what you're being told you need to do by other "leaders" and experts online.

You're posturing as an attempt to control how you're being perceived. You're spending more time pretending to be the expert than doing the work to create expertise. And you're putting the majority of your effort into positioning yourself to be seen as the expert by beefing up your website, sales copy, and messaging.

You are desperate to be recognized as a leader in your space, and that desperation leads you down the path of self-conscious leadership. You claim to know things that you don't know and are quick to regurgitate knowledge that you've yet to implement. But if you claim to know everything, you've unconsciously made the decision to stop growing, to stop learning, and to close yourself off to new ideas, new insights, and new challenges. Rather than spending time to integrate, implement, and improve, you spend your time designing a picture-perfect external image as an attempt to control how you're being seen.

Despite your best intentions, you are letting yourself be driven to fulfill your ego and not your purpose.

Potent Leadership isn't about being "the best," nor is it about being "better than" others. It's about being your best self and leading from that place. After all, we're all on the same journey; we're just at different stages of our journeys. And when you lead with that belief, you'll gain the ability to truly see and authentically connect with your audience. You'll be a true leader.

Let's be real . . . the word *leader* has lost its meaning. Thanks to social media, we see a rise in people who are claiming the status of "leader" without owning the responsibility that comes with that role. Leadership carries a vital responsibility, yet here we are, bombarded with "leaders" who look down upon us with their purchased followers, speaking *at* us with their megaphones, doing anything and everything to impress us.

THIS IS NOT LEADERSHIP.

In this old paradigm of leadership, leaders place themselves on pedestals in an attempt to create a sense of superiority.

They possess "I'm better than you" and "Listen to me because I know better" energy and an "us vs. them" mentality that has created division between humans over the centuries. And that's why this type of leadership worked—because leaders have used it to create false problems and false enemies through narratives that have led to wars between nations, wars within society, and wars between and within ourselves. It's a manipulation tactic used to position themselves as the savior—someone who is here to save you from these problems and these enemies.

Not only have we seen this pedestal leadership in politics, but we've also seen this in religious groups, cults, corporations, the health-care industry, businesses (large and small), educational systems, the personal and spiritual development industry, and social media.

THIS IS NOT LEADERSHIP.

This is self-conscious leadership. This is what happens when you're more devoted to your ego than you are to your movement. And as much distaste as you may feel for this form of leadership, I invite you to consider the fact that you may be engaging in this and showing up as a self-conscious leader.

Let me first clear up any misconceptions around ego because the spiritual industry has really given ego a bad rap. You've been led to believe that you need to somehow destroy or get rid of your ego, but that's not the case, and it's not actually possible. Ego is your sense of SELF—it's how you distinguish yourself from other people and the rest of the world. In other words, your ego is part of who you are. It only becomes problematic when you let yourself be led by your ego or let your ego dictate how you show up. It's a fine balance between being aware of your ego and making conscious choices from that awareness, and being unaware of your ego.

Sigmund Freud (the controversial and revered founder of psychoanalysis) describes ego as one of the three metaphorical parts to the mind:

1. **ID:** The id operates at a purely unconscious level and focuses on our desires, drives, instincts, and impulses.

2. **EGO:** The ego works to meet the id's needs and is grounded in reality (a.k.a. our physical, 3D world).

3. **SUPEREGO:** The superego is the part of our mind that strives to act in socially appropriate and moral ways.

Now, without diving too deep into psychoanalysis, the ego is the part of your mind that is constantly working to protect yourself, often through any means necessary. Which means that your ego can be a little defensive. In fact, because your ego is so great at its job, it's created defense mechanisms to protect you and keep you from experiencing anything unpleasant.

There are many different variations of defense mechanisms, but here are the eight most common ones (as identified by Sigmund Freud and his daughter, Anna Freud):

1. **REPRESSION:** Your ego pushes unwanted thoughts out of your conscious mind.

2. **DENIAL:** Your ego blocks unwanted, upsetting, undesired, and overwhelming experiences and events, causing you to not see, not believe, not acknowledge, and perhaps even refuse to accept what's happening.

3. PROJECTION: As an attempt to fix your problems, your ego attributes your unacceptable thoughts, feelings, and motives to another person.

4. DISPLACEMENT: Your ego will have you satisfy an impulse via a substitute person or object in a socially unacceptable way (e.g., releasing the anger that you feel toward yourself on your partner instead).

5. REGRESSION: Your ego will lead you to move backward in your development to cope with stress or overwhelming situations (e.g., acting like your eleven-year-old self).

6. RATIONALIZATION: Your ego attempts to justify a mistake, problem, or undesired feeling with seemingly logical reasons or explanations.

7. REACTION FORMATION: Your ego will lead you to express yourself or behave in ways that are opposite of your true feelings. (e.g., attempting to control everything because you actually feel insecure).

8. SUBLIMATION: Like displacement, your ego will have you satisfy an impulse via a substitute person or object, but in a socially acceptable way (e.g., channeling your frustration into your workouts).

In knowing that these defense mechanisms are built into your ego, it becomes easier to understand why ego gets a bad rap and how ego plays into self-conscious leadership. But we need our egos to ground us into our sense of self as well as our reality. So when it comes to the common spiritual belief that we need to somehow abolish or get rid of our egos, this is false. Instead, I encourage you to learn how to work with your ego and maintain a healthy relationship with self. Become aware of your ego's presence and when it flares up, and from there, make conscious choices and decisions on how to move forward. The key is to respond, not react.

Now that I've clarified the truth behind your ego, let's get back to leadership and the ways in which you may engage in pedestal leadership by showing up as a self-conscious leader.

YOU'RE ONLY IN IT FOR YOUR EGO.

You're reacting (and not responding) from your unconscious defense mechanisms to protect yourself with any means necessary.

What does this look like in action?

Reacting by arguing with people (and not responding to people) in your comment threads when they disagree with your post.

YOU SACRIFICE INTEGRITY.

You're willing to stretch the truth, pretend, and even lie to others and yourself to get the external results you seek.

What does this look like in action?

You say all the "right" things and show up in all the "right" ways without actually doing the work (e.g., sharing posed photos of yourself meditating when you're not actually committed to a meditation practice) so that you can gain the praise and attention from others.

YOU'RE DISHONEST WITH YOURSELF AND OTHERS.

You're unwilling to see the hard truths and, instead, show up in ways to paint a pretty picture while hiding the "flaws" you don't want anyone to see.

What does this look like in action?

Lying to yourself about what you're capable of doing (because you don't like to admit to yourself that you're still a student), which leads to giving your potential clients false promises in order to enroll them into your programs and services, or to sell them your products.

YOU VALUE THE TRUTH ONLY WHEN IT'S BENEFICIAL TO YOU.

You ignore or dismiss the truth when it hurts you, but you'll choose to see it when it benefits you.

What does this look like in action?

You avoid seeing the ways in which you are holding yourself back from launching your podcast (i.e., fear of failure, fear of getting it "wrong"). Instead, you keep yourself in a state of inaction by obsessing over that graphic designer who took your money, fucked up your podcast artwork, and disappeared without providing the final result, using this as the excuse to not launch.

YOU SHOW UP IN WAYS THAT PROVIDE YOU WITH WHAT YOU WANT, NEED, OR DESIRE.

You have a way of making everything about you.

What does this look like in action?

You're there for your peers only when it's in your favor, but you ignore them or are mysteriously "too busy" when they need you.

YOU'RE OBSESSED WITH THE EXTERNAL (AND NOT INTERNAL) RESULTS.

You've attached your worth, your value, and your level of success onto your external results, causing you to chase external goals, achievements, and accomplishments.

What does this look like in action?

You implement multiple strategies as an attempt to create more income because you've attached your worth to money, but you avoid doing the inner-work to feel worthy from within.

YOU'RE CONSTANTLY DOING (AND NOT BEING) AS AN ATTEMPT TO PROVE YOURSELF.

You're great at DOING and taking action and keeping yourself busy because you feel as if you have to prove your worth—to yourself and to others.

What does this look like in action?

You work long hours and believe in hustling and sacrificing yourself, your time, and your energy, but you're not letting yourself be present in anything. You believe that you need to prove your leadership rather than just show up and be a leader.

These examples are some of the ways in which you might be engaging in pedestal leadership and showing up as a self-conscious leader.

Ouch, right?

I'm lovingly calling you out because the ONLY way you'll shift into Potent Leadership is by acknowledging and accepting the ways in which you've been showing up. You cannot change what you're unwilling to see. This is the real work. It's your duty to lead responsibly because there are people who look to you for guidance. And if you're not willing to hold and honor that responsibility, you're NOT a leader.

No more pedestals.

No more speaking down to others.

No more seeing others as "less than" you.

No more reacting.

No more trying to prove yourself.

No more lying to yourself.

It's time to retire the old ways of leadership so you can enter this new paradigm and rise as a Potent Leader. If you want to keep your claim on the title "leader," do the fucking work and make sure you're truly BEING a Potent Leader and not a self-conscious leader.

CHAPTER 2:
YOUR ADDICTION

S ocial media is built to promote addiction. Every time you get notified of positive interactions on social media, such as "likes" and "follows" and "shares," your brain releases a neurotransmitter called dopamine, and you instantly feel good.

Let me make this super clear . . . dopamine is part of our internal reward system and is released when we experience feelings of pleasure or satisfaction. Your brain releases dopamine when you have sex or eat food that you crave, and it is associated with drugs, alcohol, gambling, and other addictions that give people a hit of those feel-good feelings.

The more hits of dopamine you get, the more reward pathways you create, the more you crave—hence, why you go after that second cookie or drop more coins in the slot machines. Just like with any other addiction, social media becomes another substance of abuse. All of a sudden, checking your phone becomes a habit that you just can't quit. Social media can even cause something called "phantom vibration syndrome," which is exactly what it sounds like—you think you feel or hear your phone vibrating, but it's not.

Social media creates instant gratification and instant rewards in the form of attention from your audience, with very minimal effort. Think about it . . . you have the power to give yourself instant dopamine hits with a quick tap of your thumb. This is why it can feel tough to regulate your time online. Brain scans of social media addicts are similar to those of drug-dependent brains: There is a clear change in the regions of the brain that control emotions, attention, and decision making.[1]

"According to TED, five to 10 percent of internet users are psychologically addicted and can't control how much time they spend online."[2] With a whopping 45 percent of our world's population (3.5 billion people) using social media, that means up to 350 million people are addicted!

Think about the last selfie or video that you shared online that gained a lot of positive interaction . . . Those interactions triggered a hit of dopamine, which created a neural pathway, rewarding your behavior of sharing online. Your unconscious mind now associates sharing online with feeling good, which creates a habit you continue to feed . . . because who doesn't want to feel good?

You are stuck in the Social Media Dopamine Loop, and this greatly influences the type of content you share. Instead of sharing for service, you share for your ego to give yourself dopamine hits so you can feel good.

1. Kelly McSweeney, "This Is Your Brain on Instagram: Effects of Social Media on the Brain," *Now*, March 17, 2019, https://now.northropgrumman.com/this-is-your-brain-on-instagram-effects-of -social-media-on-the-brain.
2. Kelly McSweeney, "This Is Your Brain on Instagram."

SOCIAL MEDIA
DOPAMINE LOOP

Receive "Likes"

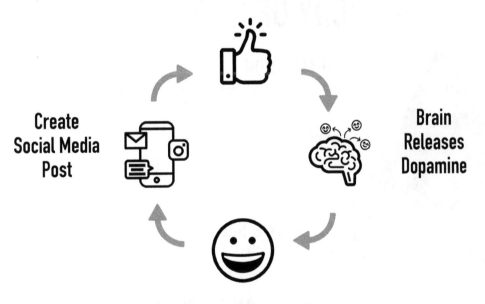

Create
Social Media
Post

Brain
Releases
Dopamine

Validation Received!
You instantly feel good.
New neural pathway created.

Now let me be clear about one thing before we go any further: Whether it's a social network, an app, or your emails—social media is any way in which you socialize and communicate with people online.

Social media has created a like-culture, and we're all living it. Remember Maslow and his hierarchy of needs? Your need for love and belonging gets satisfied by positive social feedback. You have the power to validate someone just by the tap of your thumb, and you gain that validation from others by the tap of their thumbs.

MASLOW'S
HIERARCHY OF NEEDS

SELF-ACTUALIZATION
desire to become the most that one can be

ESTEEM
respect, self-esteem, status, recognition, strength, freedom

LOVE & BELONGING
friendship, intimacy, family, sense of connection

SAFETY NEEDS
personal security, employment, resources, health, property

PHYSIOLOGICAL NEEDS
air, water, food, shelter, sleep, clothing, reproduction

This like-culture is influencing what you share (and how much you share), what you wear, what you say, how you present yourself, how you label yourself (a huge reason why labels are so important today), and who you be. All of this makes it harder for you to find your voice and tap into your potency because you're unconsciously preoccupied with getting positive social feedback so you can fulfill your social media addiction.

But what happens when you don't get those likes and hits of dopamine? You miss out on the reward and the feel-good feelings, which leave you feeling less than worthy. Your basic human need for love and belonging is neglected and you feel shitty about yourself. This can either cause you to hide from social media or push even harder by sharing with the sole purpose of getting those dopamine hits. And maybe you find yourself doing a combination of both . . . hiding AND pushing dopamine-inducing content. It's a vicious cycle that is diluting your potency and making it harder for your ideal audience to find you.

If you're treating this like a numbers game, you'll lose sight of the fact that behind every single "like" is a human being who tapped the like button. Behind every single "share" is a human being who tapped the share button. Behind every single "follow" is a human being who chose to follow you. And yet here you are, obsessed with gathering more "likes," more "followers," more "engagement"; and this obsession with numbers is killing your potency and disconnecting you from the people in your audience.

Social media has become the killer of all things social and has, in fact, created an anti-social society. You can see this clearly when you go out to eat. Just look around and notice how many people are sitting together but are on their phones. Couples on dates engage more with their phones than with each other. Families eat out, yet are completely disengage with each other because they're all on their phones. It's also become a distraction that is used to fill space. Think about that the next time you pull out your phone while in line to pay for your groceries.

Social media is meant to be SOCIAL, but it's now become a twisted version of a seventh-grade popularity contest. You crave the dopamine hits and will do anything and everything to get them . . . even if that means manipulating your words and showing up in fake AF ways.

The hidden truth in all of this is that despite all the dopamine hits, you don't actually feel good. It takes more energy to dilute your potency and sacrifice your truth in exchange for the numbers. Feelings of anxiety increase, you struggle to show up, and you seek a better way—you just don't know what that looks like. You've created a habit of scrolling and staring at that glass screen, and this habit is fueling something toxic, something I like to call "comparisonitis."

Do you suffer from comparisonitis?

If you've ever felt like shit after scrolling your feed, that's a sign that you do. In fact, scrolling fuels comparison, which triggers feelings of depression.

What you need to understand is that what you're witnessing online is a series of people's highlight reels—carefully curated content, shared to fulfill an identity that has been chosen by the person sharing. After all . . . isn't this what you do?

It's easy to feel less than enough when you're seeing nothing but highlight reels. It's also easy to feel disconnected and alone in your misery—as if you're the only one who isn't where you want to be, doing what you want to do, achieving what you set out to achieve. Comparisonitis is the ultimate potency killer.

In a session with my client Mateo, he shared with me his vision of empowering people by creating inspirational video content. And yet, he was holding himself back from making it happen. We'd create the goals together, he'd feel excited for a day, and then comparison would hit, and he'd get caught up in trying to make things perfect because deep inside, he felt less than enough.

What Mateo didn't realize is that he was comparing himself to leaders who have been creating and sharing video content for years! He wasn't seeing what went on behind the scenes, or the team of people who created the videos, or the years of effort and practice that went into it, and he placed an expectation on himself to produce content of similar quality from day one.

Mateo was stuck in an external feedback loop, unconsciously seeking validation through social media. He was plagued with comparisonitis and this deeply impacted his ability to show up consistently for his purpose. When this was uncovered in one of our coaching sessions, something shifted. Mateo saw with absolute clarity all the ways in which he was holding himself back from showing up due to his "need" for external validation. He was ready to break free from his habit of comparison and get shit done—to prove to himself that he could do it.

And then it happened . . . I received a message from him with a video attached. Mateo created and shared not one but two videos in a span of two days and he felt amazing about it! Not because of the positive social feedback that the videos were receiving, but because of the sheer fact that he created a new story for himself—one that had him creating the validation he sought from within.

This is what it all boils down to . . .

> ▶ Are you willing to give up your addiction for something greater?
>
> ▶ Are you willing to fight through your comparisonitis for your vision?
>
> ▶ Are you willing to do whatever it takes to get your message out there?
>
> ▶ Are you willing to leave the like-culture behind and be a Potent Leader?

CHAPTER 3:
INFLUENCERSHIP VS. LEADERSHIP

All leaders are influencers, but not all influencers are leaders. The difference between the two is motivation and intention. They both have influence, but leaders are motivated by their purpose with the intention to serve their vision and community. Influencers are motivated by their ego with the intention to serve themselves.

Let's talk about influence. Lexico dictionary defines *influence* as "the capacity to have an effect on the character, development, or behavior of someone or something, or the effect itself."[3] So, the truth is we all carry within us the power to influence. But what motivates you to use that power? What's your intention behind that power?

Ego is a tricky thing. As I shared in chapter 1, you need ego, yet when you lean too far into ego, you'll inflate your sense of self-importance. The spiritual development industry has shunned ego to the point where many people believe that it's a bad thing and they don't need it. But that's far from the truth. You need your ego.

---

3. Lexico, *Oxford English Dictionary*, s.v. "Influence (*n.*)," accessed May 3, 2020, https://www.lexico.com/en/definition/influence.

But when you lean too far into your ego, you start to develop an enlarged sense of self, which influences your thoughts, choices, actions, and presence. This can happen to the greatest of leaders. Leaders with the best intentions and beautiful motives can suddenly fall into the trap of seeking external significance, approval, and validation because they have yet to find these within themselves. Social media makes it far too easy for you to lose sight of what's truly meaningful to you, all by tempting the parts of you that are craving to be seen, heard, acknowledged, and understood.

This is when you fall onto the path of influencership.

I understand the temptation. I've received countless invitations to become a brand ambassador, "rep" a company's products, or simply share products on Instagram in exchange for cash, free products, or a shout-out. But do such brands or products actually align with me or you, your values, and your purpose?

This is where motivation and intention come in. For example, the influencer who is motivated solely by ego (to feel significant) and who has the intention to serve themselves (to feel seen) will say yes to opportunities even if they aren't fully aligned with their values or purpose. They'll say yes because they're seeking that false sense of credibility and significance to overcompensate for the lack of credibility and significance they feel within themselves.

But the leader is different. The leader who is motivated by their purpose and who has the intention to serve their vision and community will only say yes to opportunities that are fully aligned with their values and purpose, while turning down all other opportunities. Alignment is key to leading with integrity.

When it comes to influence, you may think that you need to rep bigger names and brands to be perceived as credible or important or a leader with clout, but that's your ego talking, trying to compensate for how you truly feel about yourself.

Being an influencer may reward you with shiny toys, swag, media, and other opportunities, but being a leader will fulfill your purpose. And in return, you'll still receive rewards that are fully aligned—rewards that will support you in the direction of your vision.

We were living in the era of the influencer—an era that valued image over integrity, followers over community, and perception over connection. It was a giant, superficial popularity contest that rewarded those with perceived notoriety—a contest that many leaders got caught up with because of their unfed need to feel loved and accepted, to feel a sense of significance, approval, and validation from the outside world.

Influencership isn't about who you're being—it's about how you're positioning yourself to control how you're being seen. The higher the follower count, the more you were seen as a credible authority. Influencers don't care about cultivating community—they care about boosting their follower count. This obsession with followers ignited an entire micro-industry of agencies promising to double, triple, or 10x your follower count . . . all it takes is a payment and *poof* . . . you instantly have more followers.

Everything that is offered on social media is built to feed the popularity contest, including the likes, the follows, the comments, and the algorithm to the coveted blue check mark.

People became fixated with attaining the magic blue check mark because, somehow, this check mark offered a sense of credibility, significance, approval, and validation . . . so much so that people began to share their own avatars with photoshopped blue check marks because they were desperate to be seen as credible.

Influencers hold the mindset of "what's in it for me?" and that mindset determines their actions and how they choose to show up online and offline. They are willing to sacrifice their integrity for the numbers because they're chasing superficial results. Influencers are willing to trade authenticity for whatever they need to do to get more likes, follows, gigs, interviews, stages, and notoriety.

And let's face it . . . anyone can claim to be anything. All it takes is a crafty Instagram bio, heavily produced YouTube videos, purchased followers, a few logos slapped onto a website, and *voila*!

But now things have shifted . . .

We "were" living in an era where influencers were winning the popularity contest, but now, the world can see clearly. We're no longer living in an era where influencers can gain success through the traditional ways of influencership. Humanity is seeking real support, leadership, and guidance from leaders who feel genuine with their motives—leaders who are showing up to serve their communities, and not solely their egos. Humanity is seeking Potent Leaders.

Influencers paint a pretty picture, but leaders pave a path.

We've officially entered an era where leaders, not influencers, will be the winners.

The veils have been lifted and people are seeing clearly. I've noticed more and more leaders becoming aware of how they've gotten caught up in the ways of influencership.

I remember being in that space—of feeling like less of a leader because I didn't have "enough" followers and I wasn't part of the "cool clique" in the personal development industry. I was trying really hard to fit in with the influencer crowd and had managed to connect with some well-known names in the industry, but our friendships lacked depth, and I never quite felt like I was accepted by them because of my low follower count and budget YouTube videos. I would be invited to certain events, but not the official influencer events, such as book launches with press and media—events where your follower count mattered. And yes, this definitely fucked with my worth.

I hated going to parties and events with influencers who were more fixated on posting pictures together on Instagram versus actually connecting with each other. I hated having shallow conversations with people who were more interested in what was in it for them versus having real, deep, and meaningful conversations. And I hated how influencers judged who they would connect with by their follower count.

I hated all of it. And yet, there I was, playing the same damn game.

My primal need for love and belonging was at play and I was desperate to be accepted by the cool kids of the industry because I wanted to be seen as a credible expert. I thought I was leading, but I was bypassing the real work it takes to BE a leader.

This never sat well with me. I constantly found myself torn between wanting to be seen as popular and credible, and a burning desire to blaze my own trail. After playing this game for a couple of years, I started to break free to create my own path. I had no idea what that path looked like. All I knew was that I needed to find alignment within myself, my message, my purpose, and my leadership. Chasing the cool kids was completely out of alignment.

Making the shift out of the influencer game and into Potent Leadership did not happen overnight. It was a deep journey of getting real with myself and auditing my actions: of letting go of people, programs, offers, and pieces of my business that I had built out of desperation to become "popular" and liked. I had to face my shit head-on and own the fact that I was chasing significance, approval, and validation through my presence . . . and that is not an easy thing to own.

The biggest shift for me was trusting my own path because it felt completely unknown. No more following in other leaders' footsteps, and no more people-pleasing to keep myself feeling "safe" and "liked." I put on the blinders and began blazing my own trail to unleash my potency. There was no formula or strategy other than following my own fire. As I began to shift, my business slowed down, and I gave myself more space to uncover what it was that truly lit me up.

I said "Fuck it" to the influencer game and made the conscious decision to BE a leader instead. No more bypassing the inner-work—I was in it, devoted to my unique path, purpose, vision, and mission, and I was ready to do it all in a way that felt aligned with my potency.

Once I made that shift, everything began to flow: clients were coming to me with ease, I was effortlessly creating over six figures a year, I was aligned with my values, and I felt incredible . . . like a weight had been lifted off my shoulders. It felt easy to show up because I was no longer showing up to impress—I was showing up for me, my purpose, my community, and my gifts.

This is a shift that many leaders are going through right now—including you. The pretty picture that's been painted by influencership is now being seen as the facade that it's always been. The world needs a path to follow, one that can only be paved by those who are willing to drop the facade and lead by example.

The era of influencership is dying. No more shortcuts to success, of falsely representing who you are and what you've achieved. No more bypassing the real work it takes to be a leader. Now, leadership is all about who you're being.

Fuck the blue check mark. Fuck the popularity contest. And fuck the obsession with followers. You're devoted to creating an impact by being the fullest expression of your purpose, vision, mission, and movement. You're ready to step into the NOW era of leadership by being authentic and leading with integrity so you can create longevity with your movement and loyalty within your community.

The only question left to ask you is this:

> ▶ Are your actions launching you on the path of leadership? Or influencership?

THE INFLUENCER	THE LEADER
Serve their ego	Serve their purpose and community
Image over Integrity	Integrity over Image
Numbers over Intimacy	Intimacy over Numbers
Followers over Community	Community over Followers
Seeking to gain popularity	Seeking to create connection
Focused on manipulating how they're being perceived	Focused on creating congruence (lead by being)
Seeking significance, approval, and validation	Stands with conviction in their presence
Leads by manipulating how they're being seen	Leads with authenticity
"What's in it for me?" mentality	"What's in it for my community?" mentality
Constantly seeking shortcuts	Focused on creating a legacy
Prefers to be in control	Practices self-trust

You might think you're being a leader, but if you're spending more time crafting perfect social media posts to serve yourself than actually leading and serving your purpose, you are chasing influencership.

I remember once hearing Rich Litvin say: "If you're a coach who's spending more time writing social media posts than coaching clients, you're not a coach—you're a marketer."[4]

Did that feel like a gut punch? Because it definitely felt like one when I heard him say that. I was spending a lot of time marketing myself to serve myself, and not my community. I was getting caught up chasing likes and follows and popularity—all of which was leading me further and further away from my potency.

Influencers focus on serving themselves. And this can happen to the best of leaders because our digital world rewards those with higher follower counts and blue check marks.

But you can be a leader and still reap rewards without losing your potency. As a leader, you can serve your purpose, grow your community, and receive external rewards with integrity, all while remaining aligned with your values and your message.

Buying farmed followers is easy, but it's also the quickest way to throw yourself out of alignment and integrity. Leadership is about committing to the journey of uncovering who you be. It's about becoming the fullest expression of your mission, your message, and your movement. It's about leading by being, not preaching. It's about serving your purpose and your community and knowing that by doing so, you will also serve yourself.

> ▶ In what ways are you showing up as an influencer?
>
> ▶ In what ways are you showing up as a leader?
>
> ▶ What actions are you ready to take to make the shift from influencer to leader?

---

4. Rich Litvin, coach, advisor, and author of *The Prosperous Coach*, http://richlitvin.com.

CHAPTER 4:
SIGNIFICANCE, VALIDATION & APPROVAL

You're caught in the trap . . . Seeking significance, validation, and approval through external sources.

You're sharing what you're sharing on social media because you're seeking the approval of your audience and perhaps even your peers. But this pattern also leaves you feeling depleted, uninspired, and like an imposter.

You're creating what you're creating because you're seeking to validate your gifts. But this pattern also has you underpricing your programs, products, and services, which leaves you feeling resentful and unappreciated.

You're caught in a cycle of "do more," "hustle more," and "achieve more" to prove yourself. But this cycle has left you feeling burnt out and as if nothing is ever good enough.

What you must realize is that you've trapped yourself, and the only way out is IN.

You're chasing significance, validation, and approval because you have yet to approve of yourself, validate yourself, and find significance within yourself. As human beings, we all share the basic human need for love and belonging, and if we don't feel that sense of love and belonging, we will unconsciously seek it out with whatever means necessary because our brains see this as a need for survival. Your chase for significance comes from a deep need for survival.

Your trauma, your wounds, your history . . . all this programming in your unconscious mind influences your actions, thoughts, and identity. You've trained yourself to seek what you need through external sources. And there's no need to feel ashamed of this . . . in fact, drop the shame right now, because we are ALL seeking significance.

The reason you're in this trap is that you're seeking that sense of significance through external sources. But the truth is . . . you'll never find the significance you seek as long as you are on this external chase. The significance you seek can only be established within you.

You must get yourself to a place where you truly understand the importance of yourself, your life, and your purpose. You must accept yourself, for all that you are. You must tap into that love within you. You must get yourself to a place where you KNOW you matter. This is the work that you GET to do. After all, leadership begins with you leading your life. It begins with you consciously creating the life that you live, instead of just letting life drag you with it.

Imagine what would become possible if you were to establish significance within yourself—letting go of the need to prove yourself to others or be approved by others . . .

▶ How would you show up?

▶ How would your messaging shift?

▶ How would your energy shift?

▶ How would your leadership shift?

These are the shifts that you get to create.

It's time to get yourself out of the trap by finding the significance you seek, within you.

Let's consider how this need for external validation probably started. As a child, you trained yourself to seek what you needed through external sources because you weren't getting it from the people around you.

I remember being told that I could do better each and every single time my report card came around. And I remember hearing my dad praising my middle brother for the plethora of As on his report card . . . leaving me to believe that unless I got As, I was not good enough for my dad.

BOOM. My nervous system was rewired with a new belief.

"In order to be loved and accepted by my dad, I need to get As on my report card. If I don't get As, I will not be loved and accepted by him."

This is just one of the beliefs that caused me to train myself to seek that validation and approval through external sources because I wasn't getting it from my dad.

Since our unconscious minds see our desire for love and belonging as a need for survival, my unconscious mind decided to take matters into my own hands so I could survive. So even though this is a false belief, as a child, it served me because it protected me from feeling unloved and unaccepted.

No matter how false a belief may seem, it's embedded in your unconscious because, at some point in your time line, it was serving you by keeping you safe. This is how easily we create these beliefs. And now, you're left with the responsibility to rewire those false beliefs into beliefs that actually serve you. So, ask yourself . . .

My client Jess was in the final week of launching her group coaching program and was starting to feel burnt out. She explained to me that she left her calendar open for potential clients to book enrollment calls, which left her with no time for herself. When I asked her why she chose to leave her calendar wide open, she paused, took a couple of minutes to reflect, and then replied, "Because I want people to find a time that works for them so we can get on these enrollment calls."

I then proceeded to ask her what would happen if she didn't keep her calendar wide open, and she replied, "I wouldn't fill all ten seats of my program."

"If you didn't fill all ten seats of your program, what would that mean about you?" I asked.

She said, "If I don't fill all ten seats, who I am to coach these clients? I'd feel like an imposter."

I then witnessed Jess having a light bulb moment—a moment that would forever shift the way she approached her goals.

Jess realized that she was attaching her worthiness to the accomplishment of her goals, and in this specific experience, her worth was attached to the outcome of filling all ten seats in her coaching program.

As soon as she communicated her light bulb moment with me, she shifted. She then proceeded to create time-blocks for herself in her calendar, shortened her enrollment call windows, and even reached out to two of the eight potential clients she had booked calls with that week, asking them to clarify a few answers on their applications because from the answers they initially submitted, she didn't feel they were an aligned fit. She had originally booked these calls with them out of desperation to fulfill her goal, therefore validating her sense of worthiness.

And maybe you can relate . . .

> ▶ Do you validate your worth through the outcome of your goals?

▼ ▼ ▼

Self-worth is an inner-game. But when you start chasing your worth instead of uncovering it, you start to lead your life and purpose with ego. There are leaders who lead with ego and leaders who lead with heart. *Which one are you?*

It's time for a massive reality check—and this one may sting a little. Trust me, I know because I've had to experience it for myself.

In the first few years of building my coaching business, I was leading with ego. I didn't realize it specifically back then, but I felt something was off. I didn't always feel good about what I was sharing, creating, and building. There was always this voice in the back of my head saying, "If you don't achieve this, there's something wrong with you."

When I didn't achieve the specific outcome, I set for myself—such as selling out my events, filling my group programs, or getting invited to speak at an event where all my peers were speaking—I'd crumble. I would have a breakdown, cry, eat chips, watch trashy reality TV, and have myself a big-ass pity party.

Eventually, I'd get myself back up. I'm a high achiever . . . it's what we do. Yet I'd continue to find myself in that same cycle . . .

Share-create-build.

Feel as if something was off.

Not fulfill the expected outcome.

Break down and have a big-ass pity party.

I was stuck in the trap, and I couldn't even see it. And I'm certain that if someone had pointed it out to me and said, "Hey, Ruby! You're stuck in the trap because you're leading with your ego," I'd reject what they said and resent them for saying it.

After all, I was claiming to be a heart-centered leader. How could I possibly be leading with ego?

And then it happened . . .

I can't remember the exact post that I shared, but I remember the feeling I had when I shared it.

It felt gross. I realized that I was sharing what I was sharing because I was desperate for someone to validate what I was going through . . . rather than doing the inner-work to validate myself.

Once I saw that, the fog lifted, and I started seeing ALL the ways in which I was leading with ego and chasing significance, validation, and approval through external sources.

Going into debt to produce one-hundred-person events so I could feel significant.

Creating a digital course to prove that I was an "expert" in my industry.

Sharing vulnerable posts not to serve, but to validate my worth.

Connecting with the "popular kids" in my industry to seek their approval.

The proof was everywhere. I was leading with ego and it pained me to acknowledge that I was doing this. But through the acknowledgment and acceptance of my current behavior, I was able to create a shift and get myself out of the trap.

Think about it . . .

> ▶ WHY are you sharing what you're sharing?

The posts that you edited way too many times before you hit "publish" . . .

The overly edited or overly planned photos . . .

The videos that took ten-plus takes to get "perfect" . . .

The shares that start with "Vulnerable post alert!"

You're sharing in this manner because deep down inside, on an unconscious level, you're trying to validate your worth, gain approval from others, and feel significant—like you matter. And the only way you believe you'll achieve this is by manipulating your truth. Whether you're aware of this or not, THIS is the reason why you feel trapped.

You've attached your worth to the outcome.

You're not aware of when you started doing this, but now, after reading this, you've realized that you're depending on specific outcomes to validate your worth.

You're caught in the trap and it feels like shit.

First things first . . .

As a fellow self-judgment expert, refuse to beat yourself up over this. The fact that you're now seeing this attachment is the first step to getting yourself out of this trap.

You are exactly where you need to be. Awareness is key.

Every single outcome that you've been chasing—whether it's filling your program, selling a certain number of products, gaining a certain number of followers, speaking on a specific stage, getting those podcast interviews—

You've been chasing validation.

You are basing your sense of worth on the achievement of these outcomes. Meaning . . . if you don't achieve these specific outcomes, you'll deem yourself as unworthy.

> ▶ Are you willing to admit that you've been chasing external validation and approval?

The fact that you're reading this book means that you're ready to step into Potent Leadership, but I want to make one thing clear. . .

This book won't change you. Only YOU can change you, and that begins the moment you take responsibility for who you are, where you're at, and what you're doing. Which means it's time to own your shit. So, it's time to get real with you about something.

Your desire to be known as a "leader" is actually a desire for significance.

You're not alone. I've felt this too, as have the hundreds of leaders that I've worked with. This is why you're working your ass off, hustling to get clients and customers, getting certification after certification, burning yourself out, and struggling to feel aligned. Your desire to be known as and seen as a leader is really a desire to feel significant—to feel important, accepted, and loved—to feel as if you matter.

Consider all the things that you are currently doing to establish your expertise:

What you choose to share on social media, who you choose to hang out with (or better yet, be seen with), the certifications and training opportunities you choose to pursue, the goals you choose to go after . . .

Take a moment right now to list these things out. And then, ask yourself WHY.

- ▶ Why do I choose to share what I share on social media?

- ▶ Why do I choose to be seen with the people I'm seen with?

- ▶ Why do I choose to pursue the certifications and trainings that I pursue?

- ▶ Why do I choose to go after the goals that I'm going after?

Again, you're not alone. Many people on our planet are seeking some level of significance to compensate for the lack of acceptance they feel in their life. But very few people are willing to dive deep, face their shit, and accept the fact that their actions and how they choose to show up are influenced by their desire for significance.

This is where you step in—the Potent Leader—the thought leader on a mission to change the world—the human being brave enough to do the inner-work necessary to show up as the leader you know you're here to be.

With this new awareness comes the opportunity to shift your pattern and create changed behavior. You can't change where you've been, but you can change where you are. By doing so, you gain the power to create a new story for yourself—a story that has you feeling significant, important, loved, and accepted, knowing that your life and your purpose matters.

You are on the path to unleashing your potency.

CHAPTER 5:
FAKE AF

Are you tired of hiding your truth while trying to fit an image of who you think you need to be?

Let's get real.

It's exhausting trying to be something you're not! And yet here you are, stuck in a pattern of being fake AF.

You're filtering yourself because you're too afraid to show up in your potent truth. And to be honest, you may not even know what your potent truth is, because you've been filtering yourself for so long.

But you're here, reading this book for a reason. You are tired of filtering yourself. You yearn to speak your truth. You yearn to unapologetically stand as the leader you are. **You yearn to be you** . . . but you have no idea where to begin.

In order to uncover the first step, you need to rewind to when your fake AF pattern first began. At some point in your journey, you realized that you'd gain more by being someone other than yourself.

I remember my journey . . . feeling the pressures of my culture to show up a certain way, to speak a certain way, to have a certain type of career, and to uphold the status of our family by not doing or being anything that could bring shame to our family name.

Even today, I can still hear my parents say things like . . .

"Don't cry!" when I cried.

"Just smile" when I didn't feel like smiling.

"Make sure you say hi nicely" when we were greeting family or family friends and I wasn't feeling well.

"Don't say that" when I shared what I was really feeling.

"Because I said so" when I questioned their demands.

My habit of filtering myself was born out of a deep desire to feel loved and accepted by my parents. I started being who they wanted me to be, saying what they wanted me to say, and acting how they wanted me to act so I could gain their love and acceptance.

Simply put, I was keeping myself safe by filtering myself. But this habit was disconnecting me from my truth and diluting my potency.

I remember the exact moment I realized I needed to filter myself to keep me and my family safe. I was eleven years old, and I had just been molested by a complete stranger.

I was shopping at the department store with my mom. I asked her if I could go look at hair elastics a couple of aisles over from where she was, and she said yes. I walked over to the aisle and started browsing the hair elastics when I felt a hand grab my chest, and then another hand pushed firmly on my mouth.

"I have a gun. If you yell, I'll kill you," he whispered in my ear.

I froze. I had no idea what was happening. All I knew is that I was scared for my life. This man continued to place his hands all over me, groping me and touching me in places I knew I shouldn't be touched with one hand over my mouth. All the while I was standing there motionless—frozen in fear. What felt like hours only lasted a few minutes. In the end, he whispered, "Don't tell anyone," and then ran off.

I instantly broke down in tears and yelled for my mom. She came running and found me in that aisle with the hair elastics, looking disheveled, heaving, with tears running down my face. I hugged her tightly and said, "A man just tried to kidnap me!"

You see, at this point in my life, I had no idea what had just happened. When she took me to talk to security, they called the police, and I was interviewed in a small, sterile security office in the mall. I explained what happened, shared that he told me he had a gun, and when they asked if he touched me in places he shouldn't have, I whispered "yes" with my head down. I felt embarrassed to admit that in front of this police officer and security guard that I had never met and ashamed to admit that in front of my mom. I turned and saw the look on her face—one of fear—and I knew immediately that she somehow felt this was her fault.

We drove home in silence, and that night, we sat in the living room with my dad to share what happened. I sat in the single chair, my dad on the big couch, and my mom on the love seat. She proceeded to explain to my dad (in the best way she could) what happened—and the whole time, her head was hanging with shame. The look on my dad's face went from anger, to shock, to sadness, to shame.

After a few minutes, my dad said: "Ruby, don't tell anyone about this."

That was the moment I knew I had brought shame to my family. And to keep my family safe from the judgment of others in our cultural circles, I needed to keep this a secret.

That was when I took my habit of filtering myself to a whole new level.

I share this story with you to paint a picture of how deeply embedded your filtration habit can be.

Maybe you experienced a trauma that left you feeling as if you needed to show up a certain way just to be safe.

Maybe you trained yourself to filter your truth after being punished for speaking it.

Maybe you started hiding pieces of yourself when those pieces of yourself were being judged by others.

Maybe you realized you'd get more attention by acting like someone else.

We all have stories from our past, and those stories play a huge impact on how you choose to show up today. Because at the end of the day, you're simply doing your absolute best to stay safe. This is a primal need, and one that all human beings share. We instinctively do things to stay safe. It's called self-preservation, and it comes in many different forms. In this case, it's showing up as a habit of filtering yourself.

But this habit is diluting your potency and negatively impacting your role as a leader. You know this because you feel this. You're exhausted from trying to be what you're not. You're tired of keeping up appearances—feeling one way yet showing up in a completely different way. You admire those who seem to effortlessly show up unfiltered and in their truth. You want to be like them and embrace your potency. But that begins with you letting go of the need to filter yourself.

To kick your habit of filtration, you must first answer the following questions:

> ▶ In what ways are you filtering yourself? Be specific.
> ▶ What do you fear would happen if you didn't filter yourself?

> ▸ What is your habit of filtration costing you (i.e., aligned clients, real friendships, freedom, emotional well-being, and so on)?
>
> ▸ What would it look like to be unfiltered? Be specific.
>
> ▸ How would it feel to be unfiltered?

Answering these questions won't remove the habit from your unconscious mind, but it will help you see the truth behind the habit and feel the possibility that comes from kicking the habit. When you feel the possibility, you create an imprint in your unconscious mind, making it easier for you to replicate in real time.

As I've mentioned throughout this book, it's up to you to do the inner-work. Your habit of filtration won't kick itself to the curb—you have to do that. Answer the questions, face your shit, and open yourself up to feeling the possibility of being your unfiltered self.

Let's evaluate what you get from this fake AF version of yourself. You've created a false identity based on what you *think* your audience wants. You're doing everything and anything to keep up appearances so you can be perceived a certain way.

→ You're filtering your truth by sharing only what you think will garner you more "likes."

→ You're showing up in inauthentic ways to appease this false identity that you've created for yourself.

→ You're posturing yourself to be seen as an "expert" or "leader" because you're desperately trying to build credibility.

→ You're engaging in manipulative tactics to achieve the results you want.

But what are you really getting from all this? Does it feel good? Or has it left you feeling lost and confused about who you are and what you have to offer?

What I want to make super clear here is that your fake AF behavior may not feel fake or manipulative to you just yet. You might be reading this, thinking to yourself, "I'm not being fake," but hear me out.

The photos and videos that you choose to share . . . Do they REALLY represent you? Or are you over-filtering yourself to be perceived a certain way?

The content that you publish . . . Are you writing in your true voice? Or are you editing your words to appease the masses?

The presence that you choose to embody when speaking on stage or attending events . . . Are you truly being yourself? Or are you trying to be seen as someone you're not?

As hard as this may be to admit, you're being fake AF and it's hurting your leadership.

What you're failing to see is that you're not giving your real audience an opportunity to find you. Your fake AF ways are preventing them from seeing the real you, creating a massive disconnect that is actually pushing the right people away.

You're not attracting the "right" audience because you're not offering them a chance to connect with you—the real you. You're filtering yourself, you're posturing, you're editing your words and wearing a presence that isn't truly your own. This is why you've attracted an audience that feels misaligned—an audience that isn't actually interested in your services or offers.

Your habit of being fake AF costs you your ideal audience.

→ Maybe you've found yourself blaming your audience for only wanting your free shit.

- → Maybe you've found yourself blaming social media's algorithm for not getting the results you seek.
- → Or maybe you've found yourself blaming the oversaturated marketplace for not getting more eyes on your movement.

But the real problem here is you. You're not letting your audience see you, hear you, or feel you. The "right" audience for you is one that is aligned with you, your values, your vision, and your movement.

You've got it backward if you're trying to align yourself with your audience. Your ideal audience is meant to align with you.

This was a lesson that I learned after trying to fit my perception of an "ideal" audience. I was constantly struggling to fill my coaching programs and attract aligned clients—clients that I truly felt passionate about serving. And then at the end of 2018, I hit a wall with my health issues and took a step back from everything to spend a year completely devoted to my inner-work.

During that year, something interesting happened. Since my main focus was my health and well-being, I started to show up less online and stopped attending live events completely. I became a hermit—devoted to healing myself in the deepest of ways, sitting in psychedelic plant medicine ceremonies every month, and eventually heading to the Amazon jungle in Peru for a fourteen-day plant medicine dieta where I was completely disconnected from everything, dieting psychoactive medicinal plants and trees while living with the absolute bare minimum (more on this later).

Throughout this year in solitude, spending less time online and more time inward, I uncovered my voice. My entire journey since hitting rock bottom in 2012 has been a journey of uncovering my voice, but 2019 was truly the year where my voice amplified because

I reconnected to my potency. This was only made possible because I spent less time scrolling and seeing other people's content and more time diving deep within myself.

I got ideas for coaching offers that felt incredibly exciting, and I mapped out a vision for how I wanted my life, business, and movement to look and feel. I launched The Activation Retreat and filled it effortlessly, with the most aligned clients and leaders . . . just by showing up as me. I launched The Thought Leader Collective—a concept that I had for a couple of years but was too afraid to launch—and filled it effortlessly, with the most aligned clients and leaders . . . again, just by showing up as me. I literally filled all my coaching programs for 2020 by February 2020 . . . effortlessly.

I exchanged my habit of being fake AF for a habit of being real. I let people see me, hear me, and connect with me . . . because I was finally in a place where I could see myself.

No more tactics.

No more posturing.

No more manipulation.

The leader I am today is 100 percent congruent with the person that I am . . . and that's the secret very few people seem to understand.

I've also witnessed this happen with my clients . . . going from struggling to fill their programs to having ideal clients reach out first.

The reason you're not attracting the "right" audience is that you're too busy being fake AF. This means that the ONLY way to attract the "right" audience is to be real AF.

Your ideal audience exists. You just have to give them an opportunity to find you.

If you're spending all your time trying to blend in with others, how is anyone going to find the things that make you who you are? The reasons they want to work with you, specifically?

You lose pieces of yourself every time you try to mimic what others are doing. Whether you're aware of this or not, your habit of scrolling is influencing you to act in ways that are not true to who you are.

→ You see a certain type of marketing strategy work for another leader, so you mimic it but fail to get the same results.

→ You see a certain style of video work for another leader, so you copy that style but the video lands flat with very little views or engagement.

→ You notice how a certain leader with a big audience shows up, so you try to show up like them, using their language and replicating their image, but your audience doesn't grow.

And throughout all of this, you're feeling less and less like yourself. You're diluting your potency. In fact, you're losing sight of who you truly are and are feeling disconnected from your voice. You feel lost.

To be fair, you've probably been doing this unconsciously—unaware of the fact that you're trying to be like "them." But now, after reading this, my hope is that you become aware because it is through this awareness that you'll gain the power to create change.

It's time to start focusing on showing up in ways that ultimately feel really good to you . . . by being you.

Think about all the leaders that you truly admire—the ones that stand out to you. They stand out because they're being true to who they are. They have their own unique quirks and behaviors . . . they have their own style and energy . . . they have a voice that feels like their own . . . and they're congruent in all ways (what you see is what you get).

Don't get caught up with trying to find what makes you unique. What makes you unique is the accumulation of ALL that you are— your voice, your presence, your purpose, your style, your mannerisms, your quirks, your shadows, your light, your message, and your gifts. THIS is your potency.

> ▶ At the top of a fresh new piece of paper, write "Who am I, really?" and bullet-point everything that comes to mind. Let yourself free flow without questioning or judging anything that comes up. Just write.

CHAPTER 6:
YOUR FALSE IDENTITY

Why do you choose to filter yourself? Why do you hold back on speaking your truth or showing up as the person that you truly are? At what point in your life did you start feeling unsafe to be you?

My client Chanée left her home at age eighteen. From there on out, she taught herself to fight for her success, to prove to herself that she was worthy because, in her mind, her worth was determined by her external success *(sound familiar?)*.

This translated into her working hard (but not smart), over-extending herself to her clients, and losing herself in her work. As a result, she began to posture herself to be seen a certain way, edit herself to fit an expectation of who she thought she needed to be, and filter herself to please those around her, including her clients and her audience.

Chanée was wearing the many masks of **PEF** (posturing, editing, and filtering) because she felt unsafe to be her. She grew up believing that the feeling of worthiness that she desired could not be achieved by being herself, so she created a false identity to chase worthiness by achieving external results, such as enrolling clients, earning a certain amount of money in her business, and gaining a certain number of followers.

Does any of this sound familiar? You may have a different life story, but the reasons why we wear these masks are always the same . . . We are all seeking a sense of love, belonging, and safety.

You might be thinking, "I understand the need for love and belonging, but why safety?"

Safety isn't just about having a safe environment—safety is about predictability and creating certainty and experiencing familiarity. There is a part of you that is always seeking to know "for sure" because this helps you feel safe. Here's how this may manifest in your mind:

"I want to know for sure that I am liked."

You want to feel certain that you'll be liked, which means you'll do anything and everything to please those around you, which might include editing your words to match theirs and filtering your image to fit their expectations.

"I want to know for sure that I won't be judged."

You want to feel certain that people won't judge you, so you'll hold back and may even hide, even when you feel called to show up.

"I want to know for sure that I'll be successful."

You want to predict your success, but since this type of predictability is hard to achieve. So you hold back on taking action and may even keep yourself in a state of stagnancy due to a fear that you won't be able to create success.

"I want to know for sure that it's possible to create wealth by pursuing my purpose."

You want to feel certain that by pursuing your purpose, you will create the financial freedom you desire, so you follow those who seem to have what you want, and you posture yourself to be like them and mimic what they're doing in hopes of achieving what they've achieved.

"I want to know for sure that all of this is leading me toward my vision."

You want to predict your future. You want to know that all of this is leading you somewhere, and you'll do anything to feel that level of predictability, including listening to all the "gurus" and experts, following their advice (even if it goes against your values), and posturing yourself in a strategic attempt to fast-track the journey to your vision.

These are the many masks of PEF, and each time you wear them, you lose more and more of your potency.

Which leads me to an exercise for you.

> ▶ Grab your journal and write out as many "I want to know for sure . . ." items as come to mind. Don't over-think it; just write. And don't judge yourself as you write; just write. It's time for you to get clear about the safety that you're seeking and the ways in which it's driving your behavior and actions.

> ▶ Have you finished the exercise? What did you find? My guess is you noticed that you're hiding behind a false identity. You're afraid to show the world who you truly are, and this fear has led you to create layers upon layers of masks that you've taken on as your identity. But this falsified identity is having a negative impact on your life, business, and movement.

Let's be real . . . it takes a lot of effort to be something you're not. And the more you pretend, the more disconnected you become from your true identity and potency. In fact, there's a chance that right now, you have no idea who you truly are. This is the reason why you're struggling to attract the right people into your business and movement.

You're posturing as an attempt to control how you're being perceived.

You're editing yourself to please your audience and impress your peers.

You're filtering yourself because you don't feel worthy enough to be seen as you.

You are hiding behind the many masks of PEF, and you may not even be aware of it. Let's break this down.

WHAT IS PEF?

LET'S START WITH POSTURING.

As the Oxford Dictionary so eloquently describes, posturing is a "behavior that is intended to impress or mislead."[5] And most people engage in this type of behavior without even realizing it, including you.

Whether you're fussing over the perfect "look" to impress or you're behaving in ways to make people think you're something that

---

5. Lexico, *Oxford English Dictionary*, s.v. "Posturing (n.)," accessed May 17, 2020, https://www .lexico.com/en/definition/posturing.

you're not, this type of behavior not only misleads those around you, but it also misleads you from truly understanding who you are.

I remember my very first speaking opportunity. It was 2016 and I was nervous as fuck. Not only was this my first speaking gig, but I was speaking alongside a crew of powerhouses: influencers, and leaders who I had placed on pedestals. I watched as they each took the stage, oozing confidence and charisma, engaging with the audience in ways that blew my mind . . . and my nerves continued to intensify. I was paying attention to how they were showing up, how they stood on stage and walked through the crowd, and how highly energetic they were. I thought to myself, "I need to show up like that in order to be taken seriously."

To be honest, I felt like a total imposter next to the other speakers and questioned whether the audience would value what I had to share. This led me to question my behavior and my energy. I'm not naturally as animated as they were on stage but they were the "experts," right?

After watching a few speakers on stage, I went backstage to collect my thoughts. I knew that if I were to posture myself to be highly animated like them, I wouldn't be authentic to myself. I started rehearsing, amplifying my energy to match theirs, forcing myself to make grand gestures with my arms as I spoke (which isn't natural for me), and I became more nervous. This did not feel like me at all, and in fact, all this posturing was throwing me off my game.

They called my name to let me know that I was up next. My heart sank into my stomach. "Am I really going to do this? Can I be like them?" I thought to myself. The speaker before me was wrapping up his speech as I stood next to the stage when I felt an overwhelming urge to take off my heels. So, I removed my shoes.

I went up on stage and spoke barefoot, mostly grounded in one place on the stage, not overly animated, but I felt 100 percent me. I was in my flow—something that would not have happened if I was posturing. And you know what? At the end of my speech, I received a standing ovation. People were in tears and the feedback I received from the audience was so heartfelt. Funny enough, someone in the audience commented on how different my energy was from the other speakers and that they appreciated my grounded presence.

I share this story with you because the choice to posture yourself is always available to you. You can always shift your behavior to impress or mislead. But when you choose to stand in your potency, that's when you give people an opportunity to really see you and connect with you—the real you.

I've also noticed posturing take place at the events that I've spoken at across the world. Many leaders choose to show up only for their slotted speaking time and hold back from truly engaging with the audience before and after their speech. Instead, they'll hide out at the back of the room, making it tough for people to connect, or they'll leave the room or event altogether. Why? Because of the old paradigm of leadership that places leaders on pedestals, which is similar to creating a sense of "celebrity status." So, they posture their behavior to be seen in that way—as a type of celebrity.

Posturing is also something you might be doing to mislead yourself into thinking you are something you're not. This is something I see often with the leaders I've worked with.

Maybe you're trying to convince yourself that you are someone who can "hustle hard" to achieve your goals, but when you do hustle, you burn yourself out.

Or maybe you're trying to convince yourself that you are someone who can wake up at 4:00 a.m. and start your day early with your morning routine, but when you do, you feel exhausted, depleted, and unable to focus by 2:00 p.m.

Or maybe you're trying to convince yourself that you are someone who can share live videos online every single day, but when you do this, you find yourself sharing content that feels misaligned, diluted, and incredibly forced.

Your habit of posturing is pushing you further away from your potency, making it tough for you to create the movement you know you're here to create and serve the people you know you're here to serve. Not only are you misleading your audience, but you're also misleading yourself.

NEXT UP IS EDITING.

Have you ever felt as if you needed to edit yourself when speaking to others? To change what you would normally say in order to please or impress them? If the answer is yes, you know just how exhausting it is to constantly be editing yourself.

You overthink everything you say, share, talk about, or post, and you overanalyze your words to the point where you no longer understand what it is that you want to communicate. It's almost as if you can never get it right, and you find yourself spending way too much time writing a single piece of content because you're so wrapped up in pleasing your audience.

It's frustrating to feel as if you can't say what you want to say and share what you want to share. It's also incredibly taxing on your energy to constantly be thinking twice about everything. And often, you'll find yourself in a state of pretending versus a state of truth because you've edited yourself so much that you've completely lost your potency.

As a child, I was constantly told what to say and how to act. My natural words and actions didn't align with who my parents and our cultural society expected me to be.

"Don't say that!"

"Say this . . ."

"You can't do that!"

"Do this . . ."

And if I went against the instructions that were given to me, I wouldn't be accepted by others. In many situations, I would be seen as "bad" or "wrong" or like the black sheep of the family. So, I adopted a habit of editing myself to gain acceptance from those around me.

I bit my tongue a lot and edited myself when I spoke to others, which only contributed to my anxiety disorder. This behavior and my anxiety continued into adulthood. At the end of the day, I just wanted others to like me, and in many situations, I wanted to impress people into thinking differently of me. And eventually, my habit of editing myself became so ingrained into my being that I suppressed my real voice, even to those who I deemed close, in fear of being judged, disliked, or abandoned by them. I was editing myself around my friends, my boyfriends, my family, and my coworkers in order to be perceived a certain way because that's who I thought I needed to be so I could be loved and accepted.

I know you've experienced something similar . . .

→ Biting your tongue to hold back on sharing how you really feel because you're scared that by doing so, you'll no longer be loved.
→ Editing yourself in conversations to impress those around you so you can receive their approval.
→ Spending way too much time overanalyzing and changing your content before you hit "publish" because you so desperately want to feel accepted by your audience.

You're suppressing your voice and you're adding to your anxiety when all you truly want to do is be yourself, even if you don't fully understand who you are. You crave the freedom that comes with saying what you want to say, sharing what you want to share, and doing what you want to do, because right now, it feels as if you're living your life as someone else.

FINALLY, WE HAVE FILTERING.

In the digital world that we live in, filtering can be taken to a whole new level. Let's start with the vanity filters that we have available to us with just a tap of our fingertips. Back in the day, you had to use programs like Photoshop to filter your photos, but not anymore. Vanity filters have become much more accessible. Instagram started this social media rage back in 2010 with its release, giving users the option to add filters to their photos. But since then, vanity filters have exploded, with myriad options available, such as presets, AR filters, and thousands of apps that allow you to perfect your images from the convenience of your phone.

Look, don't get me wrong, I love a good filter or preset, and I'm not discouraging you from using them. I'm encouraging you to understand your relationship with filters. Are you using them because you don't feel good enough to be seen without them? Have you become so addicted to vanity filters that you cannot share an image or video without them? Are you tying your self-worth to your physical appearance? Think about it.

Another type of filtering is the behavior we program ourselves to do. Filtering your words, thoughts, and opinions because you don't feel worthy enough to be heard or seen as the person you are. Whether you're saying 75 percent of what you really want to say, or 50 percent, or 5 percent, you are filtering yourself because of your worthiness wound. It's like you're giving your audience and those around you only a small portion of you.

My client Jen struggled with this in her business. Growing up and living in a part of the US that was heavily Christian, Jen didn't feel comfortable speaking about spirituality. In fact, she didn't even feel comfortable owning the fact that she was incredibly spiritual due to the programming of her environment. But she was. Jen loved her tarot cards and crystals; she loved studying the goddesses, releasing emotions through ecstatic dance, and grounding through breath work and meditation. She had built a spiritual backbone but hadn't fully owned that it was there.

Looking at Jen's business, her online presence, and her stage presence, you would never know that she was as spiritual as she was. Sure, she wore a set of crystal beads on her wrist, but she never spoke about it. In fact, when Jen and I first connected, I had no idea. Instead, Jen had created a false identity and didn't even realize it. She was playing the role of the strong, masculine, fired up, hustle-hard coach when reality, she felt most like herself when she was in her yin energy of grace and flow.

Things hadn't clicked for her in her business for years. She felt like she had tried everything, reinventing herself and her messaging often, all the while filtering out her truth in fear of being seen as "too woo" or "crazy" by the people around her. Jen felt like she needed to filter out this part of her in order to be taken seriously by her ideal clients and audience, when in fact, they needed to see the real her, "woo" and all.

While working with me in the Thought Leader Collective, Jen stopped hustling and started diving deeper within herself. She started to go after the things that felt really good and let go of the things she thought she should be doing. And through it all, she began to drop more into her true self, embracing her yin energy. She began hosting intimate events for women online where she unleashed her spiritual self . . . and these women loved it! They loved learning about the goddesses and spirituality and ecstatic dance, and Jen felt more lit up than ever.

The filter was coming off, and soon, Jen began to show up online in the fullest expression of her potency. Her fear of being seen as "too woo" had dissipated. Instead, she owned her spiritual nature and finally gained the clarity she had been chasing and yearning for in her business. She finally knew who she was, who she was here to serve, and what she was here to do. And today, Jen is living life with no filter, loving her business, and enjoying the depth of freedom she's cultivated from within.

The many masks of PEF are holding you back from experiencing the freedom of your potency. Whether you're posturing as an attempt to control how you're being perceived, or editing yourself to please your audience and impress your peers, or filtering yourself because you don't feel worthy enough to be seen as you . . . these masks are keeping you from seeing the real you.

And in order to be seen by others, you need to start by first seeing yourself.

CHAPTER 7:
ALIGNMENT

How do you want to feel? In your life, your leadership, your business, your presence, and your movement?

Society has trained you to focus on what you want to do and accomplish, but how do you want to *feel*? And are you feeling that right now?

I was the ultimate goal-chaser, and to be honest, I still am. But today, I choose to go after goals that feel aligned with who I be. Growing up, my parents raised me to have goals, and often, their goals for me became my goals because I wanted to feel loved and accepted by them—I wanted to please them.

I went to college, worked in the financial industry, got married young, and followed the path they encouraged me to follow. But something was off. No matter what I achieved or how much success I created, I never felt fulfilled. It felt like I was doing just for the sake of doing, and chasing things that didn't really feel like things I wanted to chase.

I was living in misalignment with myself and, like most people living in misalignment, I didn't even know it.

Fast-forward to 2014 when I first started my coaching business. I started this business because it felt purposeful and right, but soon after my launch, I started chasing after other people's dreams again.

I got caught up in what everyone else was doing in the coaching industry and started following their path because I wanted what they had—or so I thought.

→ I chased their goals of having consistent $10K months.
→ I chased their goals of being featured on podcasts and stages.
→ I chased their goals of having multiple offers and services.
→ I chased their goals of scaling my business.

In my first year of business, I gained over thirty features, interviews, and podcasts; I offered group and one-on-one programs, built a large and highly engaged online community, hosted webinars, built a YouTube channel, and established a reputation for myself as a leader in my niche, which, back then, was self-love. But something was off . . . I didn't feel good, and I couldn't quite place my finger on what it was that was throwing me off.

I was chasing an external vision of what I thought I needed to have to be successful when that wasn't truly what I wanted. Yes, I wanted success. But what I didn't know was that the version of success that I was chasing was not *my* version of success. On the outside, I looked successful. I managed to achieve more than most online entrepreneurs and coaches within one year of starting my business.

I was ranking on the first page of Google when you searched for "self-love" or "self-love coach." My community was building rapidly and, without any ad spending, I was enrolling consistent clients, and people were consistently asking to interview me.

But again, I felt like something was off . . . like I wasn't being myself.

This is what it feels like to be out of alignment. On the outside, things can look great. But on the inside, you feel as if something is off.

We've been trained to DO and to accomplish external goals. We've been shown a certain image of what success looks like. We've been taught to prioritize how we're being perceived. We've been told what we should go after, and who we should be.

But when were you ever taught to understand what's important to YOU?

When were you ever taught to uncover what you value? And what feels meaningful to you?

When were you ever taught to understand why the fuck you are here, doing what you're doing, chasing what you're chasing, and being who you're being?

The reason you're not feeling good or fulfilled is that you're chasing someone else's path. You have yet to do the inner-work to really understand who you be, which is why you're walking the path of others, doing for the sake of doing, chasing dreams that aren't really yours.

Most of my clients experience this prior to working with me. They build businesses that have some level of external success but are left feeling as if they're tethered to their work. They come to me feeling drained, depleted, and disconnected from what they're doing and creating. They find themselves sacrificing a lot and compromising more than they want to, and they continue to do this because they believe they must to achieve their current vision of success. And the worst part is that they feel as if they're constantly trying to fit themselves into their business when in reality, their business, purpose, and movement need to fit THEM. But they won't know how to do that unless they take the time to understand who they be.

If something feels off, it's off. Trust that feeling. This is about you getting back to a place of self-trust—of listening to your gut—of following what feels right for you and not for others. This is about you, following your own path.

The key to creating alignment in your business and movement is to first create alignment within yourself, so you can stop sacrificing your needs and stop compromising your values. You need to understand who the fuck you are and why the fuck you're here—THIS is how you achieve alignment.

And that feeling of fulfillment that you so desperately want? That can only be achieved through alignment. Your integrity as a leader depends on your ability to remain aligned within yourself.

> ▶ Why are you sacrificing so much? And for what?
>
> ▶ Why do you find yourself compromising so much? And for what?
>
> ▶ And how are you left feeling afterward?
>
> ▶ Is the vision you're chasing even yours to begin with? Or is it an image of what you think you need to chase in order to be perceived in a certain way?
>
> ▶ Is the definition of success that you're carrying actually your definition of success? Or is it something that you picked up along the way?
>
> ▶ Is the person you're being today actually who you want to be?

These are the tough questions that you get to ask yourself right now so you can acknowledge the misalignment in your life. And once you've answered those questions and acknowledged how you have been showing up, ask yourself the following questions to step onto your aligned path:

> ▶ What's really important to me?
>
> ▶ What feels meaningful to me?
>
> ▶ How do I want to feel?
>
> ▶ Who do I want to be?

And make sure everything you're doing and creating is in alignment with your answers.

CHAPTER 8:
REDEFINING LEADERSHIP

The internet has graced us with the power to see all sides of the truth—to see multiple perspectives and viewpoints. With that power, we've gained the ability to see through the veils, the masks, and the perfection. We can sense when we're being lied to, and we can feel when something is amiss. We've now become truth-seekers as opposed to compliant followers. We've developed a craving for authenticity and integrity. We feel seen when we witness transparency. We soften when we observe humility. And we applaud congruency in action.

This is why it's time for us to redefine leadership.

You're reading this book because you feel called to lead differently. You know that there's a better way to show up and serve—a way that doesn't require dishonesty, manipulation, or pedestals. You've been mimicking the ways of the pedestal leader because that's what's been modeled for you. But it doesn't feel right.

Mimicking others won't help you stand out—it will help you be like those you are mimicking. I remember one of my earlier mentors asking me about my vision: "Where do you see yourself in five years?" he asked.

I didn't even need to think about my answer because I knew exactly what I wanted my path to look like. I blurted out, "I want to be as big as Gabby Bernstein!"

He nodded his head as he slipped into deep thought. After a few moments, he asked, "But what if you're meant to be bigger than Gabby Bernstein? What if you're limiting yourself and what's possible by declaring that you want to be just like her?"

I sat back. I wasn't expecting to hear that, and it took a couple of minutes for that to register. My mind was racing: "What if I am meant for more? What if I am meant for something different altogether? Am I limiting my potential?"

That was the moment I realized that I get to lead as me, that I get to do this MY way, that I get to design my own vision. I didn't know how to do this, nor did I even have a full understanding of who I was and what I wanted. But there was a sense of freedom in knowing that I didn't have to be like anyone else.

Looking back, I see the path that I paved (not followed) to make this shift within myself and my leadership. I realized that in order to do this my way, I needed to pave this path myself and knock down my own pedestal. But because I know how difficult it is to pave your own path, I'm going to share mine with you. This path to conscious leadership is one that you can follow, and I encourage you to also make it your own.

This is the path of the Potent Leader and the beginning of the demise of your pedestal.

ACKNOWLEDGE

You cannot change what you refuse to acknowledge, which is why this is the first step. Acknowledge the ways in which you've been engaging in pedestal leadership. Acknowledge the ways in which you've let yourself be led by your ego. Acknowledge how you've been showing up.

ELIMINATE

It's incredibly tough to lead your way when you're constantly bombarded by the voices and presence of self-conscious leaders. It's crucial to your growth that you eliminate anything or anyone that may deter you from your path. Unfollow, unfriend, or mute unconscious leaders in your feeds. Disconnect from the unconscious leaders in your life. Remove yourself from any groups or communities (online and offline) that distract you from your path. Give yourself the space you need to find your own way.

UNDERSTAND

Once you've eliminated the voices of others and created space, it's time to understand who you be. Just like relationships with others, you get to cultivate that relationship with yourself. Get real with yourself about your needs, your beliefs, your fears, and your values. Use your discernment to understand who you are beneath the projections and expectations of others and the external world.

LEAN INWARD

To understand is to lean inward, and leaning inward is a practice that Potent Leaders must devote themselves to. This step isn't temporary—it's a permanent piece to your path because you're constantly evolving. And as you evolve, so will your purpose, your message, your voice, and your presence. Lean inward and listen to yourself, connect with yourself, and do the inner-work to unleash more of your potency.

CLARIFY

As you get to know yourself at a deeper level, you'll find ways to clarify your purpose, your vision, and your messaging. Just know that this is a process. The clarity that you seek may not come all at once; rather, it's an evolution—an unfolding of sorts. The more you understand who you be, the more clarity you'll create.

EXPRESS YOURSELF

You won't find your voice or establish your presence overnight. But you have to start expressing yourself to drop into your fully expressed self. The more you share your voice, the more you'll get to know your voice. The more you share your presence, the more you'll understand about your presence. Start by sharing yourself as you are today, knowing that your expression will continue to evolve as you evolve.

REPEAT

The path to Potent Leadership is cyclic and constant—it's meant to be repeated over and over and over again. And the more you repeat this, the more potent your leadership becomes, because you become more potent.

I encourage you to take this path and make it your own, knowing that you truly can't fuck this up. Potent Leadership is about leading with awareness, so all that's really required is to open your eyes and be willing to see. Kick your pedestal to the curb, be brave enough to do things your way, and use your courage to show up and lead as you. To do that, we first need to recognize what's been missing.

Having worked with hundreds of leaders around the world and having hired many leaders as my own coaches and mentors, there are five crucial traits that I've found to be missing in the old paradigm of leadership (self-conscious leadership): authenticity, congruency, humility, integrity, and transparency.

Let me break it down for you . . .

AUTHENTICITY

Self-conscious leaders lack *authenticity* because they feel they need to show up in a certain way to be perceived as a leader. They place that pressure upon themselves to be "perfect" and get it "right," while wearing masks to blend in or hide any self-perceived flaws.

> *What does this look like in action?*

> You spend way too much time trying to perfect a social media post because you want to ensure you come across as the expert. You push yourself to show up with a smile, even when you're not feeling well or are going through hardships because you don't want to be perceived as "less than" a leader. You stretch the truth (and may even lie) on stage, in interviews, with peers, on social media, or with clients and potential clients because you're so afraid of being seen as an imposter.

CONGRUENCE

Self-conscious leaders lack *congruence* because they prioritize their image over embodiment. They talk a lot but lack the action to back it up because they're in such a rush to be seen as a leader.

> *What does this look like in action?*

> You prioritize content creation over inner-work—sharing your message without fully living and breathing that message. You preach about things like meditation and breath work and

self-care, but you aren't consistent with those things yourself. Simply put . . . you talk the talk, but you don't walk the walk.

HUMILITY

Self-conscious leaders lack *humility* because they overcompensate for what they don't know, in fear of being seen as anything but an expert. They hate to admit when they're wrong.

What does this look like in action?

You pretend to know things that you don't or claim to know more than you do because you believe that in order to be seen as a leader, you need to know everything. You don't acknowledge when you've fucked up and may even try to cover your tracks or hide your mistakes.

INTEGRITY

Self-conscious leaders lack *integrity* because they get caught up with the numbers. They obsess over collecting "likes," "follows," and sales because they attach their worth and sense of significance to the outcome, and they let that obsession influence their actions.

What does this look like in action?

You purchase followers as an attempt to improve the optics of your social media accounts. You overpromise to get people to buy, but underdeliver on the product or service.

TRANSPARENCY

Self-conscious leaders lack *transparency* because they're afraid of being seen. They're afraid of being seen because they have yet to fully see themselves.

What does this look like in action?

You constantly mask your true emotions because you don't want people to think you're weak or incapable of doing what you're here to do. You avoid working on your own shit and instead hold a "high-vibe" demeanor when seen in public (online or offline) because you want to be perceived in a positive light.

These are the five missing traits in leadership, and they are the foundation for Potent Leadership. What you need to understand is that when you lack these traits, you're not leading anyone because you have yet to truly lead yourself.

Leadership is an inner-game—it begins within. You must become the fullest expression of your purpose, your message, and your vision. You must model the possibilities that you speak of by being it. And you must do this by owning your shit, admitting when you're wrong, speaking the truth, walking the walk, and being real.

Your entire life, you've been praised for doing what you're told, such as listening to authorities and obeying the external rules, regulations, and systems. And you're punished for doing otherwise. Everything in our material world is created to train you to comply and obey, including street signs and traffic lights and rules and regulations.

But at some point, we all wake up and realize that we're caught in a trap. And I'm guessing, since you're reading this, you've felt that wake-up call and are starting to see this trap—the trap of significance, approval, and validation.

As a leader, authority is important. But when you're in a constant race for external authority, you're not truly leading—you're chasing. We were never taught how to build authority from within.

What you need is inner-authority—to love yourself, to trust yourself, to believe in yourself, and to feel worthy for who you are. You were trained to trust the world but not yourself. You've been trained to master external authority, making it easy to believe that everything you need can be found through the external world. But this chase for external authority will have you on the run for your entire life.

It's time to find what you're seeking from within you so you can show up as the Potent Leader you know you're here to be.

Potent Leadership begins with having the authenticity, congruency, humility, integrity, and transparency to courageously lead your mission and draw people into your movement. These traits are what make you human, and it's time to bring humanity back into leadership.

The people you're here to serve are hungry to see YOU—not a picture-perfect version of you. They want to see you, but they can't if you aren't brave enough to be seen as the human that you are.

Gone are the days of the self-conscious leader. It's time for a new paradigm for leadership, and that paradigm begins now, with you and your inner authority.

CHAPTER 9:
WHY THE FUCK ARE YOU HERE?

What's really driving you to step into leadership? Your heart? Or your ego?

When you first chose the path of your purpose, you were driven by your heart—by your desire to help others and serve your mission. But somewhere down the line, you lost sight of all of that, and your ego began to take the wheel.

So let me ask you this. . .

Why the fuck are you here?

Do you remember? There's a chance that you've evolved since you first started this journey, which is why it's important to revisit this question. Understanding why the fuck you're here will help you create a real connection with your community while staying true to your path. It's the thing that will keep you grounded in your purpose. When the path of influencership seems more attractive, this will tether you back into alignment.

Understanding why the fuck you're here makes it easier for you to connect with your community, but it will also help you connect with yourself. Understanding why the fuck you're here will help you reignite your potency because it will help you drop into alignment with yourself. This is the beginning of your shift from leading with an influencer mindset to leading as a Potent Leader.

> ▶ Why are you running your business?
>
> ▶ Why are you pursuing your purpose?
>
> ▶ Why are you creating content?
>
> ▶ Why are you building a community?
>
> ▶ Why are you creating a movement?
>
> ▶ Why are you pursuing leadership?
>
> ▶ Why does this matter to you?

Once you have these answers, it's up to you to make the shift. You must audit your online and offline presence, your programs and offers, your social media bios and posts, and your messaging. Everything needs to align with why the fuck you're here. Everything needs to align with your heart and not your ego.

No more chasing significance, approval, and validation. This is about you rising into leadership, taking ownership of your purpose, and letting yourself be seen. The leader isn't here to prove anything—the leader is here to be the fullest expression of their purpose and vision.

You didn't choose this path to become popular. You chose this path to create an impact for the people who need it most. And you're here to pave that path for the people you're here to serve.

From here on out, make choices that align with you—choices that bring you closer to the fulfillment of your purpose and not your ego.

When Chanée first came to work with me, she was running a fitness coaching business that she resented. She had more than twenty clients and was overworked, exhausted, and underpaid. What became clear to me immediately was that there was a massive misalignment in her business because she was leading by appeasing the masses.

Chanée had an incredibly unhealthy relationship with social media, one that had her scrolling for hours each day, comparing herself to others in her industry, leading herself down the path of self-deprecating thoughts. What she didn't know was that deep down inside, she was seeking the significance, approval, and validation of others through their likes, comments, and follows. She had unknowingly enrolled herself in the popularity contest and was in a race to win. This race had her cutting corners; she was bypassing the real work to understand herself. Instead, she was taking the easy and safe route as an attempt to become known. She was sharing vanilla content, attracting and enrolling misaligned clients out of desperation, creating programs and offers to please the people in her audience even though they weren't her ideal clients, and offering deep discounts due to her fear of not being "enough."

When we first started working together, Chanée didn't really know her ideal audience because she didn't really know herself. She didn't recognize her gifts because she was fixated on the validation of others. Chanée desperately wanted to become a known expert but was chasing credibility without actually doing the work to become a credible, known expert. She was on the path of influencership.

The deeper we dove into Chanée's personal story, the more she saw all the ways in which she was getting caught up in the influencer game. She was running her business following someone else's rule book. She didn't know why the fuck she was there, nor did she fully understand her gifts and her vision. Leadership is about leading your life first, and Chanée started doing just that. The more she understood herself, the more she started to understand her dream clients. Through our work together, Chanée created crystal clarity in her business, her purpose, her vision, and her message by getting clear on who she was first. She began to stand in conviction of what she had to offer and started to show up in the most unapologetic ways for herself and her community.

A year later, Chanée's business was completely different. She knew exactly who she was serving, and she was leading by being the fullest expression of her purpose. She was attracting aligned as fuck clients with ease into programs that truly lit her up. And today, Chanée is showing up as a true leader in her industry and has become a known, credible, and trusted expert by embracing her potency and owning her purpose.

CHAPTER 10:
THE LEADER

Congruency is the leaders' currency. It's not a currency that is earned through external sources such as the reputation of the influencer, but rather, it's created from within. You can always spot the difference between a leader who is congruent with their message and a leader who is incongruent.

Congruency in leadership happens when your actions match your words, your words match your presence, and your presence matches your values. It's about being everything that you teach, preach, and share, leaving no room for doubt. As you can imagine, congruency is an incredibly powerful currency that adds to your potency. It's also something that does not have to be spoken or explained because congruency speaks for itself.

I remember when my incongruency started . . . I was about two years into my coaching business and had gained great success, yet I was overloading myself with work. I was working with a lot of clients, producing an annual three-day event that literally took eight months each year to plan, creating content daily, hosting retreats, and struggling to keep up with my own self-care. My work had become the priority and as such, my well-being was suffering.

Me—the leader who preaches, teaches, and shares about the importance of inner-work was letting her inner-work slide. Incongruence is a slippery slope, and this was just the beginning of my downhill path.

My messaging started to become impacted by my impaired well-being because I was being inconsistent in what I was sharing. I would talk about the need to hustle one day, and then why we should not hustle the following week. I would talk about honoring your self-care while completely ignoring my own. And I found myself often creating content for the sake of creating content instead of creating to serve.

This slippery slope of incongruence left me feeling like shit. Not only was my physical, emotional, and mental health affected, but internally, I was at war with myself because incongruence goes against my number one value, integrity.

This was also impacting my business, and I started to attract a misaligned audience. And soon enough, nothing in my business felt good. I realized that I had created many aspects of my business because I felt like I "needed" to because I saw other leaders doing the same. But those aspects of my business were not at all aligned with my values.

My health started to deteriorate, and I was suffering on a physical, emotional, mental, and spiritual level, so I took a pause and decided to prioritize my well-being. I let go of everything that did not feel aligned, including a group coaching program, my one and only online course (which had taken a big investment on my end), and my three-day annual event (which was the hardest to let go because I truly loved the event, but the demand wasn't there, and the production was draining my health).

The more I let go of the things that were misaligned, the more clarity I created for myself. I dove deep into my inner-work, healing my body, mind, and spirit. I stopped paying as much attention to the online space to cut my pattern of comparisonitis. And I started to drop into alignment with what truly felt right and good for me.

In 2019, I completely redesigned my vision for my business and leadership by stepping into my potency. For what felt like the first time, I was showing up as the fullest expression of myself, in the fullest embodiment of my purpose. I was congruent in every way, so much so that I no longer felt a "need" to preach about who I am. I let my presence lead for me.

That was the same year I launched The Activation Retreat. That launch was nothing like any of the launches I had done in the past. This one was filled with ease, joy, and excitement, and for the first time ever, I felt like I was attracting the most aligned-as-fuck clients, making it easy to sell out the retreat.

Congruence is a powerful currency. It speaks for you because it's felt by those around you. Congruence is the currency that leads to integrity, which is what our world needs right now. It instantly creates a sense of credibility and makes it easy for people to trust you because you are being everything you preach, teach, and share. And it's something that greatly adds to your potency.

The more congruent you are, the more potent you become.

Another way to increase your potency is to focus on how you can best serve your community, not your ego. Leadership is about serving your purpose, vision, and mission, all of which involve the people you're here to support. And in doing so, you will receive better, more aligned rewards than you would if you were chasing influencership.

Think back to why you started in the first place. What inspired you to step into leadership? Why did you choose to pursue your purpose?

The story tends to go a little something like this . . .

You experience hardships, hit rock bottom, rebuild your life in a better and more aligned way through your own inner healing, realize that you've been chasing the wrong things for the wrong reasons, gain clarity on what you really want, uncover your purpose, and decide to pursue your purpose with the intention to support others while creating a genuine sense of fulfillment.

This is the Purpose Journey, and it's one that you chose to activate. Not everyone who goes through major life shifts decides to pursue their purpose—but you did. You're here to serve your community, and in doing so, you'll serve your purpose.

THE
PURPOSE JOURNEY

 Pursue Purpose

 Uncover Purpose

 Clarity

 Realization

 Rebuild

 Rock Bottom

This is the path of leadership, not influencership.

→ The leader places people before profit and understands that by doing so, wealth can still be created.

→ The leader's actions create connection, not division, allowing them to truly see, hear, acknowledge, and understand their community.

→ The leader shows up with integrity, and they create that integrity by practicing congruence and remaining authentic.

→ The leader is devoted to their inner-work so they can continue to show up as the fullest embodiment of their leadership.

→ The leader has a natural influence and does not have to manipulate, posture, or fake their way into the hearts of their community, because their community trusts them.

→ The leader trusts themselves fully and as such, never feels a need to control the way in which they show up.

THIS is Potent Leadership.
And this is what you're here to do.

CHAPTER 11:
PERFORMATIVE LEADERSHIP VS. POTENT LEADERSHIP

Shakespeare said it best when he said: "All the world's a stage, and all the men and women are merely players." And yet, with the rise of the digital world, we're now witnessing performances reach new heights.

We have, within us, the power to decide who we be each and every single day. And at the same time, we have the power to control how we're being perceived—all it takes is a carefully crafted bio, a carefully designed image, carefully crafted captions, and carefully selected photos or videos, and voila! You have crafted your performance.

We see this every day . . . Leaders who are fixated more on talking about and capturing what they're doing with photos and videos versus being present with what they're doing.

Leaders who prioritize being seen and recognized versus just being present with their lives and those around them.

Performative leadership is what happens when you're focused on serving yourself and not your purpose, and to be honest, it's easy to perform. It's easy to pretend and manipulate the truth in order to fit a perception of who you think you need to be. But all of that pretending and manipulating leads you to become a performer, not a leader. It's also easy to perform for your own benefit as a self-preservation technique, to keep yourself feeling safe.

But leadership is not a performance—it's a way of being. It's how you show up. It's who you be.

You must always remember: Leadership is about something so much bigger than you. You must be willing to kick your ego to the curb and do what's right for the right reasons. But that can only happen if you're willing to acknowledge that you're performing and being driven by your ego.

→ Leadership comes with responsibility.
→ Having "followers" comes with responsibility.
→ Having an audience that looks up at you and listens to you comes with a responsibility.

That responsibility means doing what's right for the right reasons (not for your ego).

You cannot perform your way to leadership. Either you're a leader or you're not. Over the last few years, it's become very clear to me that this is a rampant issue in leadership, especially in the online space where leaders have the ability to hide behind their screens, showcasing content to posture themselves because of their unconscious need to be loved and accepted—to have their worth as a leader validated by their audience.

Amid all the recent world events, I've witnessed leaders acting as if nothing in our world has changed—leaders continuing to run business as usual, as if they've chosen to turn a blind eye to the rest of the world. I've also witnessed leaders attempting to capitalize off these events, using these events as opportunities to increase their numbers instead of increasing awareness for a cause or serving that cause.

The recent world events (along with the growth of digital media) have also given rise to "shame culture" and "cancel culture," both furthering the divide and polarity found within humanity.

Shame culture is a toxic behavior used to humiliate others for their actions or inactions. For example, someone sliding into your DMs or emails and shaming you for not speaking up on a current world event or shaming you for having a different opinion. Another example of this is when multiple people start publicly shaming you online, perhaps in the comments, because they disagree with your actions or inactions. And due to your innate need for love and belonging, you may end up changing your actions to appease those who have shamed you due to the pressure you felt. But speaking up only when you feel shamed into doing so, or shifting your actions to appease those who have shamed you, is not leadership—it's performative leadership. And let's be clear: *you* can also engage in this toxic behavior by shaming those around you (whether you're conscious of this or not), which is also a form of performative leadership.

Cancel culture is when someone is shunned, shut down, blocked, or banned for having and/or sharing different opinions. For example, journalists being fired from their jobs for reporting a narrative that differs from the rest of mainstream media, or doctors being terminated for offering alternative solutions during a crisis, or even leaders being banned from social media for sharing their own opinions. All of this can leave you feeling fearful of speaking up or doing what you feel is right. But if you allow yourself to be led by the fear of being canceled, you will find yourself in a state of performative leadership.

Whether you're letting your actions be dictated by those who shame you, or you're the one doing the shaming, or you're holding yourself back due to the fear of being "canceled," this type of behavior is the exact opposite of leadership. And it's a sign that you need to start prioritizing your inner-work.

→ If you're only speaking up because you feel that you should to be perceived as a leader, you're performing, not leading.

→ If you're only using your platform to raise awareness because you feel that you need to in order to be seen as a leader, you're performing, not leading.

→ If you're only speaking up because you don't want to miss out on an opportunity to grow your audience, you're performing, not leading.

→ If you're only using your voice because you see other leaders doing so and feel guilty or ashamed for not doing the same, you're performing, not leading.

→ If you use activism in self-righteous ways to fulfill your ego instead of supporting the cause, you're performing, not leading.

→ If you're only speaking up because you feel shamed into doing so, you're performing, not leading.

→ If you're acting in ways that encourage division and polarity within humanity, you're performing, not leading.

And your performance is a reaction to what you're truly feeling within.

Whether it's a social justice issue, human rights issue, political issue, environmental crisis, or any other world event that demands our attention, as a Potent Leader, it's crucial that you don't turn a blind eye or flip this into an act of self-righteous activism, because this isn't about you. This is about doing the inner-work to dismantle your own beliefs and prejudices about the world's events so you can take real action for the cause while encouraging real conversation. All of which takes having the courage, willingness, and humility to do the inner-work, and not just talk about it.

When pivotal events happen in our world, it's crucial that you take the time to respond and not react, so you can lead and not perform. You may feel internally pressured to speak up right away because you feel that this is what you need to do to be perceived as a leader, but it's crucial that you take the time you need to ensure that you're responding to the situation, and not reacting. If you speak up because you feel pressured to speak up, or you feel ashamed for not doing so, that's on you, and you get to sit with what you're feeling versus react publicly.

What I've witnessed during these world events is a lot of leaders amplifying their own voices, their own platforms, and their own presence—fueling their own egos to make themselves feel better or feel good. I've witnessed leaders saying all the right things without *doing* the right things. I've witnessed leaders performing on their screens while bypassing the real work required to support a cause. I've witnessed leaders shaming and canceling others while positioning themselves to be the one with all the answers.

Performative leadership is what's wrong with leadership today, and it's taking place on all levels.

→ The performances in spiritual leadership.
→ The performances in new world leadership.
→ The performances in new paradigm leadership.
→ The performances in new age leadership.
→ The performances in conscious leadership.
→ The performances in political leadership.
→ The performances in our world's leadership.
→ The performances in business leadership.

And what about all the performances that take place right before your very eyes? In the palms of your hands . . . via your phones, tablets, and other devices? Again, I encourage you to acknowledge your own performances.

As a leader, you're not expected to know all the answers, nor are you expected to get it right the first time. But you've programmed yourself to believe this, which is why it's easy for you to get caught up in the performance. Having an online audience only adds to the performative behavior because now you're instantly rewarded for your performances. But this is not Potent Leadership. You think you're doing what's right, but you're not doing it for the right reasons. You're doing it to serve your ego and not the cause.

Your rise into Potent Leadership requires you to acknowledge your self-serving ways. After all, awareness is what differentiates the conscious leaders from the self-conscious leaders. And just because you have a voice doesn't mean you have to use it—it means that you get to use it consciously, which can only happen through responding and not reacting.

Events that will challenge you to speak up and do what's right will continue to happen. But as a leader, you must do what's right for the right reasons.

→ Don't just talk about it—be about it.
→ Respond, don't react.
→ Use your voice responsibly.

You're not here to perform—you're here to lead.

While we shouldn't use our platforms to react without thinking, there will be times when you are challenged to speak up on things that are difficult—times that challenge you to do what's right rather than stick to your content plan. There will be times when you will be confronted with having the uncomfortable conversations that perhaps you've been avoiding, both with others and with yourself. There will be times when you'll be called to address things that feel socially unacceptable or unsafe to address. But these are the times that give rise to Potent Leadership.

What you value matters. In fact, your values set the foundation for your leadership. The fact that you're reading this book tells me that you value integrity, and leading with integrity often means going against what's popular and taking a stand for what's right. That doesn't come without risk. When you choose to speak up on things that are difficult, socially unacceptable, or unsafe, you will lose followers and potentially clients and customers, while subjecting yourself to receive hateful comments and messages.

But NOT speaking up also comes with a risk—the risk of leading without integrity, which goes against the very foundation of your leadership. And when you show up in ways that go against your values, you will suffer the consequences of feeling and being misaligned.

Leadership is messy, and you're not expected to get it right the first time, but if you wait until you're certain that it's right, you may never speak up. And if you're worried about saying the wrong thing, know that there's a big chance that you might. But this is how we learn, grow, and evolve as leaders. You will fuck up and say the wrong thing and put your foot in your mouth. That comes with using your voice. But do not let the fear of fucking up hold you back from speaking up.

As a leader, your beliefs will be challenged, as will your opinions, thoughts, and views. You may feel as if you need to be right all the time, or have all the answers, but you don't. This isn't about being wrong or right—this is about having the humility to know that you don't know everything. And as a Potent Leader, I encourage you to be courageous enough to acknowledge what you don't know, and humble enough to admit it. I encourage you to show up transparently and to honor the fact that you are human. Because you will fuck up, you will say the wrong thing, and you will put your foot in your mouth. But with humility, you will grow from those moments, both as a leader and as a human being.

And when you find yourself in that state of reactivity, instead of jumping into a performance to save face, take a moment to pause, do your research, and think critically so you can respond.

Instead of trying to come across as an expert, admit what you don't know.

Instead of acting how you think you should be acting to be perceived as a leader, be real and be human.

> ▶ What performances are you ready to drop in order to step into Potent Leadership?

PART 2:

WHO YOU BE

CHAPTER 12:
DO YOU FEEL SAFE TO BE YOU?

H ave you ever looked in the mirror and thought to yourself, "I don't know who I am"?

I remember the exact moment this happened to me . . .

It was March 2012, and I had just ended a four-and-a-half-year emotionally and verbally abusive relationship. This was at the height of my alcohol and drug addiction, and I was devastated. In one single day, I received all the proof I needed to realize that my relationship with my boyfriend at the time had been built on a bed of lies. Multiple infidelities with women that I knew added to the deep sense of betrayal I was experiencing.

I had just kicked him out with garbage bags filled with his belongings and found myself on the floor . . . crying . . . heaving . . . barely able to catch my breath. This was my fall-to-the-floor moment. It felt like such a familiar place and I caught myself thinking familiar thoughts . . .

"Why me? Why do these things always happen to me?"

I sounded like a broken record and I knew it. For the first time, I caught myself in my victim loop. I realized I was playing the victim and feeding into a sob story . . . a story that I had continued to tell myself because, somehow, it felt easier to believe than facing the truth: I was responsible for the pain I was feeling.

And it was through that awareness that I realized that things don't just happen TO me—I choose them.

There were signs of infidelity throughout our relationship; I just chose to ignore them until I became blinded by actual proof.

No one forced me to remain in that relationship for four and a half years; I chose to stay.

No one forced me to mask my emotions through my addiction; I chose the drugs and the alcohol.

No one forced me to surround myself with toxic friends; I chose to welcome those people in my life.

I found myself on the floor, crying and heaving, feeling devastated about my life because of a series of choices that I had made! And that was the realization that changed my life forever.

I got up and went straight to my bathroom. I looked at myself in the mirror and saw a disheveled reflection of who I was.

Messy hair
Mascara running down my face
Puffy pink cheeks from crying so much
And the saddest, emptiest eyes I had ever seen

I was staring at myself straight in the eyes and had NO idea who this person was. All I knew was that this sad young woman staring back at me had to feel incredibly unworthy to have made the choices that she made to end up here.

Deep within my unconscious mind was the belief that "I am not worthy." And this belief influenced me to make choices that led me to design a life filled with self-destruction and depression, hidden behind a false identity that I created to repress what I was really feeling.

To be honest, I wasn't willing to see myself.

Up until that moment in March 2012, I resisted feeling my true emotions. I didn't feel free to be who I was because I didn't feel SAFE to be who I was.

As a child, anytime I showed my true emotions around my parents, they scolded me. "Don't cry," they said. "What will people think?" Or the worst: "Just pretend to be happy and smile."

Instead of being acknowledged for what I was feeling, I was dismissed and often shunned, making me believe that it wasn't okay to feel what I was feeling. It felt like the only time I received their love and acceptance was when I was conforming to their expectations of who I needed to be.

Around the age of eleven, after being molested and having my life threatened in public by a stranger, I developed severe anxiety and depression. I had no idea why I was feeling the depth of sadness and anxiety that I was feeling, and why it felt so uncontrollable. I was quickly given the label of being the moody child, which left me feeling completely misunderstood and wrong for feeling this way.

I didn't feel safe to be who I was. So, I began to construct a false identity—an identity that kept me safe by holding me back from experiencing the freedom to be me—the real me.

Eventually, I stopped sharing my true feelings in exchange for sharing what I thought I had to share in order to be loved and accepted. My need for love and acceptance caused me to shove my emotions deep down inside, completely repressing and dismissing what I was truly feeling and experiencing.

But when you do this, your emotions don't just go away. In fact, they get louder, heavier, and more intense. It felt unbearable to be me, so I developed coping mechanisms to keep the charade going.

At eleven years old, I started abusing ibuprofen (the only painkillers I could find in our family home). I would take up to twelve at a time and nap for hours, hoping the pain would go away. This was the start of my journey with addiction.

But addiction wasn't the only coping mechanism that I discovered . . .

I remember having a severe anxiety attack around the age of twelve. I was having what my parents assumed was "another mood swing" and they met me with resistance—asking me to calm down (which I literally could not do). I ran up into my room and sat on the floor with my back up against the door so my mom couldn't come in. She kept pushing the door, asking me to calm down and talk, but I kept pushing the door shut. I felt angry, dismissed, unseen, and misunderstood. I was blinded by my anxiety attack and had shut my eyes in anguish.

And then, I felt a sense of relief. My mom was still yelling and pushing the door, but for some reason, I felt some relief. That's when I looked down and saw that I had massive cuts on the tops of my thighs from scratching myself with my nails. The physical pain from these scratches were the distraction I needed to disconnect from what I was feeling emotionally. This was the moment that birthed my habit of self-harm.

My addictions and habit with self-harm were coping mechanisms to handle how unsafe I felt to be myself in my environment. Have you ever felt unsafe to be you? Like you might be dismissed, shunned, judged, or even unloved for being you? I think most people have at some point. And almost everyone has developed coping mechanisms. They are birthed out of your traumas as a form of protection. Whether it's addiction, self-harm, putting up walls, distraction techniques, avoidance, or anything in between . . . you are diluting your potency to protect yourself. And it's up to you to uncover what these coping mechanisms are because they are a huge piece of the false identity that you constructed.

You're diluting your potency out of a need for perceived safety. You've trained yourself to filter your truth and hide pieces of who you are because you haven't felt safe to be you. And maybe, just maybe, you've NEVER felt safe to be you.

You feel like you're trapped, wearing an identity that isn't yours.

You're conforming to be who you think you need to be, to be accepted by others. And it's exhausting.

All you want is to experience a sense of freedom, but you have no idea how to break free from this false identity that you've constructed.

You've tried chasing external solutions such as money, status, and stuff to create freedom in your life, but none of that has worked. You're still diluting your potency.

You need to understand, no one is forcing you to wear this false identity.

You can continue blaming your parents. . .

Or your ex . . .

Or your religion . . .

Or your upbringing . . .

Or your circumstances . . .

But the truth is, you built this false identity to keep yourself feeling safe. So if you don't feel safe to be you, you'll continue to feel trapped. The only way to break free from this identity is to create that sense of safety within yourself.

Here's the truth: **You GET to be you.** And that starts the moment you uncover and accept who you fucking are.

The false identity that you've been living is holding you back from being the leader you're here to be, and it's keeping you from connecting with the people you're here to serve. This identity is also keeping you from connecting with yourself because you're preoccupied with keeping up appearances. And let's be honest . . . living a false identity takes a lot more effort than living life as you. It's exhausting to posture and control how you're being perceived every day, to edit yourself over and over again to please or impress those around you, and to filter yourself to the point where you don't even recognize who you are.

This is about BEING versus "trying to be." Because when you're being who you are, there's no trying involved. This is about being the version of you when no one's around, because that's who you truly are. It's that simple, but it's not easy to achieve. If it were easy to live your true identity, you'd already be doing so. This is why it's so frustrating when other leaders say things like "Just be you!" or "Be authentic!" If that shit was easy, we'd already be doing it. Think about it. How can you lead others if you're not (or choosing not to) lead your own damn life? How can you share your message if you're not living, breathing, and being your message?

It's tough to be you because you have yet to understand who you truly are. The last time you were likely living as your authentic self was when you were an infant. You've been raised to listen and to abide by a certain set of rules and values that are not innately yours. You've been hiding behind a false identity almost your entire life, letting other people and your experiences dictate who you be. And now that you're aware of this, you get to take back control and reclaim your potency.

This is why the inner-work is crucial. You must dive deep within yourself, beneath the masks and programs and patterns, to uncover who you be. And you get to start that process now.

The love that you seek from others, it starts within yourself.

The acceptance that you seek from others, it starts within yourself.

The validation that you seek from others, it starts within yourself.

This is the inner-work. This is what you're here to do right now.

CHAPTER 13:

ARE YOU BYPASSING THE INNER-WORK?

"Nothing on this earth is standing still. It's either growing
or it's dying. No matter if it's a tree or a human being."

−Lou Holtz[6]

Nothing is permanent. Everything—including you—is con-stantly evolving, whether you're aware of it or not. Including the air that we breathe, the people in our lives, the technology that we use . . . everything evolves. Impermanence is the only constant in our world. Yet human beings are the only species on this planet who will-fully resist their evolution.

Whether you feel stuck, stagnant, blocked, or lack clarity to act, or you've gotten way too comfortable exactly where you're at, what you're experiencing is the result of your own resistance to evolution. Although you're still evolving physically (as we all are, due to our

---

6. "Lou Holtz Quotes," BrainyQuote.com, accessed April 7, 2021, https://www.brainyquote.com
/quotes/lou_holtz_629655.

biological bodies), your resistance is holding you back from creating a conscious evolution—mentally, spiritually, emotionally, and physically. You're holding yourself back from taking control of the pace and depth in which you evolve. You have this power. Everything you seek to be is within your control.

Your evolution is your responsibility.

And when it comes to your evolution, this is truly an inner-game. Don't rely on your outer world to change your inner world. The only way to take charge of your evolution is to dive inward and create the changes you seek within yourself.

Everything you seek to achieve as a leader begins with the inner-work. EVERYTHING. This is what led me to do the work that I do. By diving deep within myself, I saw firsthand how my inner world impacted my outer world. I noticed how much emphasis our society puts on the outer world—on the things that lie outside of us. I noticed how society leads us to believe that we're powerless when it comes to our evolution, and that the solutions we seek are found within external things or other people. I noticed how little we're taught to focus on our inner world, our power, and our potency. This is what I do.

You can do everything right (follow the best strategies, be trained with the best sales tactics, have an incredible team, have a beautifully designed website, have the best funnels and systems) and still be stuck exactly where you're at because you're not BEING who you need to be in order to implement and execute. You may even be chasing the wrong goals and building a business that you hate with a misaligned vision if you're bypassing the inner-work and ignoring your choice to consciously evolve.

> ▶ So, what are you chasing?

> ▶ How many marketing strategies have you imple-
> mented, only to deliver the same, undesirable
> results?
>
> ▶ How many sales tactics have you tried, only to find
> yourself, your business, and your movement in the
> same damn place?
>
> ▶ How much longer are you willing to feel stuck?
> Stagnant? Blocked? Or unclear?
>
> ▶ What will it take for you to stop chasing things
> outside of yourself to be who you know you're here
> to be?
>
> ▶ And are you willing to take responsibility of your
> evolution right now?

When it comes to who you're being in this world, you need to understand that you are not required to fit into a box. Regardless of what the experts continue to preach, you are not here to box yourself into a certain expectation, nor are you here to label yourself. You're here to be you, and evolution is a necessary part of your journey.

This truly is an inner-game, and until you start taking responsibility for where you're at, you will continue to experience more of the same.

Now I want to be clear about something . . .

This isn't a process of trying different strategies until you find one that works.

This also isn't a process of trying on different labels until you find one that fits.

This is about you taking the time to listen deeply to what it is that you truly want, and to cultivate the courage to go after it.

This is about you being you, period. Even if that means being different than who you were yesterday, because your experiences help shape you into who you are becoming.

This is about the inner-work, and this work spans far deeper than just the consumption of information.

You can read all the personal development books, listen to all the podcasts, enroll in all the courses and programs and masterminds . . . and still be exactly where you are. The shift that you're hoping to achieve won't happen on its own; it's a conscious shift that requires you to digest the information you're taking in and to act on everything that you're learning.

You need to integrate, implement, and improve. And repeat, as necessary.

I know you're in a rush to feel heard, to feel seen, to feel as though you and your work are significant. I know you're passionate about serving those you're here to serve and may even feel desperate to gain their attention. I know you're yearning to be recognized as a leader and create the success you feel you deserve. And as such, you've been learning the best strategies, reading all the books, listening to all the podcasts, enrolling in all the courses and programs and masterminds, stalking the social media accounts of all the leaders who inspire you . . .

> ▶ But are you taking the time to integrate this knowledge by shifting your beliefs?
>
> ▶ Are you taking the time to implement what you're learning by taking different actions?
>
> ▶ Are you taking the time to improve what you already know?
>
> ▶ Or are you simply on a consumption spree, rushing through your growth, acting like a sponge,

> processing little to nothing, moving from one thing
> to the next, doing everything and anything to be
> seen as a leader, only to be left wondering why you
> still feel unseen?

Social media has a way of making it seem like it's normal to achieve overnight success—to go from zero to tens of thousands of followers or to go from a nobody to a well-known expert. And while this might be true for a handful of people due to sheer luck or circumstance or pricey (and manipulative) growth strategies, it is NOT the norm.

> **"Dig into almost every overnight success story and you'll find about a decade's worth of hard work and perseverance."**
>
> —Austin Kleon[7]

It's time for you to understand that the success you're seeking is a journey, and within that journey is an exploration of self. Your personal and professional lives are not different—they are the same—because they're both rooted in YOU. This means that the journey to leadership is actually an inward journey, and not an outward one. This is so much more than just having the right marketing, strategy, and copywriting.

Having an incredible looking website doesn't make you a leader.

Having a huge social media following doesn't make you a leader.

Having thousands of people on your email list doesn't make you a leader.

---

7. "Austin Kleon Quotes," AZ Quotes, https://www.azquotes.com/author/39627-Austin_Kleon.

What makes you a leader is **who you be**. It's time to get real with yourself.

> ▶ Who ARE you being in this world?
>
> ▶ Are you in such a rush to be seen as a leader that you're bypassing the actual work to be one?

Think about it.

You want to be seen as a leader, but you're not willing to do the deep inner-work to see yourself. Instead, you're collecting knowledge but not integrating it. You're acquiring tools but aren't implementing them. You're rushing to gain more skills but you're not improving the skills you already have.

You're rushing through this journey because you're trying to prove something to yourself, instead of understanding who you be.

As a leader, you are the epitome of your work. So, make the effort to embody everything you teach. Because leadership is not about what you're doing; it's about who you're being, and this includes who you're being when no one's watching. But this isn't something that we see often. Most leaders are focused on "doing."

Doing their strategies. . .

Doing their content. . .

Doing their speeches, their talks, and their podcasts. . .

And maybe this is you.

Maybe you're caught in a cycle of "doing" because you think that this is what you're supposed to do. You're "doing" for the sake of doing because our society has been programmed to DO. And if you're not keeping yourself busy "doing" everything, you're somehow left feeling inadequate and like you're not enough. You're "doing" to claim that you're doing because this helps you validate your worth.

And somewhere down the line, you adopted a story that tells you success can only be achieved by "doing."

But Potent Leadership isn't about DOING . . . It's about BEING.

Being your purpose, being your message, being your vision . . . being the fullest expression of who you are (a.k.a. your potent self). And when you're being all that you are, there's no need to validate your worth—because you've embodied your worth. It's about being brave enough to walk through the fire before you ask your audience to do the same. It's about being the example and leading the way versus just preaching about it.

When my client Mateo and I first connected, he shared with me that he was ready to get vulnerable and start identifying the key things that were holding him back from being his highest self and performing at his full potential. He knew that he had more to give. He knew that he had more to offer. He knew that he had creativity within him, and he wanted to start putting himself out there in bigger ways. Mateo's dream was to speak on stages at huge conferences, produce consistent and inspirational video content, and impact people with his message. He was finally feeling ready to make that happen.

As Mateo and I began the excavation process in our first session, he shared with me that he used to show up consistently on social media. In fact, he had built an incredibly successful marketing agency, had produced a lot of video content (many of which had thousands of views), and had established a solid reputation for his work with clients. But then something happened that would forever change his life and his business.

Mateo was involved in a terrible car accident that resulted in a massive lawsuit. He was the victim and was left with multiple injuries that impeded his ability to walk or move, not to mention run a business. Eventually, his entire business went under as he spent the following year healing from his injuries. And due to the lawsuit, he had to stop sharing content online, including the video content, which he loved. He even had to delete some of his videos that had collected thousands of views. Since the lawsuit still wasn't complete, he felt like he was at a standstill in his life. Mateo had just spent over a year recovering physically from his accident and was ready to start building momentum again, but what became clear was that he still hadn't recovered emotionally. This accident was a traumatic event in his life, and it was time for him to face his emotional trauma.

Mateo felt like a failure, and even worse, he felt completely worthless. He was still carrying that worthlessness when we met.

So I dug deeper . . .

"Mateo, why do you want to speak on stages and create inspirational videos?"

"I-I-I want to impact people," he replied with a stutter. "Bu-bu-but I can't. I-I-I can't share videos until this lawsuit is d-done." Mateo's stutter increased as his emotions grew.

Mateo was drawn to creating a specific style of video, one that many other leaders in the online space were creating, and it would involve him on camera mixed in with inspirational music and stock footage. He was attached to this style and I wanted to know why, so I continued to dig . . .

"So, you can't impact people unless you share inspirational videos that feature you as the star?"

Mateo looked at me, eyes wide open. I could tell that I threw him off with my comment about him being the star. As we continue to dig, he realized that he desired being the star in these videos and on stages because this was how he validated that he could make an impact. The engagement on his videos was the feedback he needed to validate that he was making an impact, and the applause from the audience at speaking engagements told him that he was worthy. He was dependent on other people's feedback, and he was just realizing this now.

Mateo wanted to start producing more video content again and start speaking on stages because he was desperate to validate his worth; he was in a rush to start covering up his feelings of being a failure. We continued to dig deeper and found that this need for external validation stemmed from his childhood when he was bullied for his stutter. His entire life, Mateo had been searching for his worth outside of himself, which was why he attached his worth to his success. When his business went under, he lost his sense of worth. When he had to stop creating and sharing content, he lost his ability to chase his worth, and he was forced to be with his real feelings—the feelings that he had brushed under the rug since first being bullied as a child in grade school.

Mateo didn't feel worthy, and this was the sole reason he couldn't even see alternative ways for him to create an impact.

I offered Mateo two journaling prompts to support his shift from "doing" to "being":

I am worthy because . . .

I am enough because . . .

And he had to write this out as many times as possible, coming up with as many different answers as possible.

Mateo began to shift his self-worth. Not only that, but we also discussed ways for him to create content where he wouldn't be the star (video footage using his voice speaking over stock videos). And since his lawsuit was going to be complete in just a couple months, he could start planning to speak on stages instead of allowing himself to remain at a standstill.

What he needed to understand was that he was the one that had placed himself in that standstill. Not the person who hit him in the accident, not his lawyers who were working on his lawsuit . . . he did that. Mateo put himself in a standstill by refusing to take action toward his dream because deep down inside, he felt like a failure and didn't feel worthy enough to do what he wanted to do. And that's also what *you* need to understand. . . .

If you don't cultivate worthiness from within, you'll always be chasing it from sources outside of yourself. And when things don't work out, you'll be left feeling unworthy because you attach your worth to your external world.

The number one reason why people don't go after what they want is that they don't feel good enough to make it happen. It always comes back to self-worth. And Mateo was ready to rebuild his worth so he would be his highest self and perform at his full potential.

Fast-forward to today. Mateo has spoken to crowds of hundreds on multiple stages, is a valued leader in his company, is devoted to his own inner-growth, and truly recognizes just how worthy he is—without needing to *do* anything to earn that worth.

The biggest difference between doing and being is that "doing" dilutes your potency, while "being" strengthens it because you're embodying the fullest expression of who you are.

"Being" is about the inner-work—the work that most leaders bypass because they'd rather focus their time and energy on "doing" so they can maintain an image. They're obsessed with how they're perceived, and they prioritize image over integrity. Most leaders bypass the inner-work because they're fixated on instant gratification.

But leadership isn't like instant noodles, where you can just add water and TA-DAA! You're a leader! That's not how that works.

→ Taking a course doesn't make you a leader.
→ Obtaining a certification doesn't make you a leader.
→ Getting media coverage doesn't make you a leader.
→ And reading this book doesn't make you a leader.

Potent Leadership is about who you be. The only path to Potent Leadership is the inner-work—the process of diving inward, healing your wounds, unbecoming who you once thought yourself to be, unleashing your potency, and becoming who you are. And this work never ends, because you're constantly learning, growing, and evolving, which means that there's always work to be done. ALWAYS.

So as much as you may be in a rush to be seen as a leader, refuse to continue taking shortcuts, because when it comes to Potent Leadership, there are no shortcuts. It's about who you're being every moment of every day.

And it's not just about who you are, but about who you're growing into. You can't bypass the inner-work.

Integrate. Implement. Improve.

Information without integration is just information. But once you integrate what you learn, that information becomes knowledge. Once you implement that knowledge, it becomes a skill, a habit, or a changed behavior. And once you have that new skill, habit, or changed behavior, it's up to you to improve upon it to ensure that you don't become stagnant.

You need to *integrate* to transmute the information you've collected into knowledge. This requires you to really know and understand what you've learned versus just acting like a sponge. It's like doing long-form math versus pulling out your calculator.

You need to *implement* the knowledge into a new skill, habit, or changed behavior. This is about taking action instead of just talking about it or even worse, assuming you don't need to take action because you're "past that."

You need to *improve* upon that new skill, habit, or changed behavior. Choose to sharpen your skills, habits, and behaviors to continue being your best each and every single day. This isn't about competing with others—this is about being your best self by staying devoted to the path of mastery.

This entire process will anchor you into BEING a leader instead of just claiming that you're a leader. It forces you to be present with yourself, your shadows, and everything you're learning. It pushes you face-to-face with who you're being, making it impossible for you to fall into the autopilot ways of self-conscious leadership. And through this process, you'll also find your potency.

Is it a slower process? Definitely. There's nothing "instant" about the inner-work. It's like cooking on a stove. If you put the burner up too high, too fast, you'll burn your food. But if you find the right low to medium temperature, your food will be cooked from the inside out. The inner-work cooks up your potency, perfectly.

No more stagnancy.

No more rushing, bypassing, or cutting corners.

The inner-work is a steady process that will help you be the leader you know you're here to be. But it will invite you to confront your shadows—the parts of you that you've been resisting, neglecting, or dismissing.

> ▶ What knowledge have you yet to integrate into your life?
>
> ▶ What knowledge have you yet to really act on through implementation?
>
> ▶ And where can you begin making improvements in your life?

CHAPTER 14:
YOU CAN'T UNSEE WHAT YOU NOW SEE

You're desperate for acknowledgment . . . to be seen and heard . . . to feel validated for what you're experiencing . . . to gain the approval of others . . . to feel significant and to feel like the work that you're doing is seen as important.

You're desperate to be seen, but the truth is . . . you have yet to see yourself.

You've conditioned yourself to wear layers upon layers of masks with protective mechanisms to keep yourself from being hurt, which also keeps you from being seen. You often feel lost, as if you lack clarity, but really, what you lack is the ability to see yourself.

You're seeking visibility as a leader—to receive recognition for your work. There's a part of you that feels as if you're owed this visibility and are entitled to it. But that feeling of entitlement is really just a distraction that's keeping you from seeing yourself.

There are things that you consciously avoid recognizing within yourself (such as unproductive, stagnant habits that hold you back), and there are things that you unconsciously avoid because you've packed that shit down so deep, you've forgotten that it's there.

I'm talking about those pieces of yourself that you've been trained to feel shitty about. People have judged you, hated you, dismissed you, made fun of you, shunned you, punished you, and even abandoned you for these pieces of yourself, so you buried those pieces deep within you, and at some point, you forgot that they were there.

You've become exceptionally good at posturing, editing, and filtering yourself—wearing masks to please others while trying to control how you're being perceived. All of these as a desperate attempt to be loved, accepted, seen, and heard.

At times, it can feel downright dangerous to be seen for who you truly are. So you continue to posture, edit, and filter yourself. You continue to hide behind your masks and control how you're being seen.

But have you ever stopped and asked yourself WHY you don't feel safe to be seen?

Whether it's a fear of judgment, a fear of being misunderstood, a fear of being hurt, a fear of being shunned or punished or abandoned . . . those fears are there for a reason. Have you ever stopped to ask yourself why you experience these fears?

These protective mechanisms that you've built for yourself at one point served a real purpose—to keep you feeling safe. But now, these things are holding you back from the one thing that you're so desperate to feel—to feel seen. And the only way to remedy this is to start by seeing yourself—by getting to know who you are beneath the protective mechanisms and finding that safety, within yourself, to be yourself.

The only way you'll gain the visibility you desire is through letting yourself be seen, and that starts with you seeing yourself.

My entire family—parents, brothers, aunts, uncles, cousins—labeled me as "moody" and I hated it. It wasn't until I was twenty-one years old that I became aware of the cause of my emotional "moodiness" when I was diagnosed with an anxiety disorder. At that point in my life, my anxiety had gotten so bad that I would black out from panic attacks. And to make things worse, I had become ashamed of myself for my anxiety and mood swings. As desperately as I wanted to be seen, heard, and acknowledged for what I was feeling, I was embarrassed to be seen. Throughout my entire life, I had been shown that the depth of my emotions was not normal and, often, even laughable. And I was scared to be seen because my entire life I had been judged, ridiculed, and shamed for being me.

All of this left me feeling unsafe to be seen.

One of my favorite questions to ask as a child was "Why?" Anytime my dad would tell me that I couldn't do something, I'd ask him, "But why?"

I was taught to respect our elders, no matter what—to never question them and to always abide by them. So, you can guess just how my dad would react every time I challenged him. Eventually, I stopped asking "why" because I didn't like getting in trouble. But when you stop doing something that you're naturally inclined to do due to fear, you're telling yourself that it's not safe to be you.

For most of my life, I did not feel safe to be seen. I was shunned or punished by my parents for being me, and I was rejected by the kids at school for being me. I didn't feel safe to be me, and this is what caused me to stop seeing myself for who I was.

I was yearning to be seen, yet I failed to see myself. And I continued to avoid seeing myself until it became too unbearable to live.

But herein lies the irony,

We're all hungry to be seen, but we're afraid to see ourselves.

So let me ask you this . . .

> ▶ What's holding you back from truly seeing yourself?

Sit with that question for a minute and let it simmer.

➔ Maybe others have left you feeling as if you're not enough . . .

➔ Maybe you've been programmed to think it's wrong to be who you are . . .

➔ Maybe you're afraid of seeing something you don't want to see . . .

➔ Maybe you don't want to face the shame that you feel deep down inside . . .

➔ Maybe you don't want to confront your anger because you've been taught that anger isn't okay . . .

Whatever the reason (or reasons), you now have a habit of people-pleasing that runs so deep, you've become unconscious to the fact that it's influencing your actions and your presence.

But once you take the chance and face the person in the mirror for who they really are, you can't go back. You can't unsee what you now see.

This is a truth that became more and more obvious the deeper I went into my inner-work. Prior to 2012, I was pretty much blind to my own shit. I didn't see all the ways in which I was contributing to and even creating the chaos in my life. I was playing the victim—blaming everyone and my circumstances for the quality of my life. But my fall-to-the-floor moment changed everything, because that was when I finally opened my eyes to see how my choices and decisions had led me to rock bottom.

Not my parents. Not my family. Not my culture, religion, or upbringing. Me.

I found myself at rock bottom due to a series of choices and decisions that I willingly made. However unconscious those choices and decisions were, I chose them. I had been living my life on autopilot, as a victim, blind to my own shit.

When I finally opened my eyes and became willing to see who I was being, I saw a lot. I saw my weakened self-worth, I saw all the ways in which I was playing the victim. I saw my habit of self-sabotage, I saw my poor choices and bad decision-making, I saw my pattern of numbing out with drugs and alcohol . . . I saw it all. And once I saw all of that, I couldn't unsee it.

That's the beauty and sometimes torturous nature of this work. **You can't unsee what you now see.** Meaning, once you gain the ability to see something, what you do with that becomes a CONSCIOUS choice. You're no longer running on autopilot or living your life unconsciously. You become self-aware. But what you do with that awareness is up to you.

You can choose to consciously ignore what you now see, or you can choose to consciously create change.

I chose to create change. I chose to work on my self-worth, stop playing the victim, and take back control of my life.

The inner-work helps you build self-awareness; it helps you see all facets of who you're being so you can face your shadows, heal your trauma, and deal with your shit head on. The inner-work helps you take ownership of your growth. And the more you grow, the more you know.

What about you? You have the awareness to choose to read this book, so you have the awareness to see where you're fucking yourself up, and it's about time you owned that shit.

> ▸ What are you unwilling to change?
>
> ▸ How are you still getting in your own damn way?
>
> ▸ Where are you fucking yourself up?

You can't control how people treat you (or have treated you).

You can't control your past circumstances.

But you do have control over how you choose to proceed. You can continue to replay the same damn stories over and over again, play the victim, point the finger, and deny the fact that you are fucking yourself up . . . or you can take a cold, hard look at your life and the choices that led you to be who you are today, standing where you stand today.

"Why am I finding it so difficult to simply use my voice, speak, and just be me?"

That was a text message I received from my long-term one-on-one client, Luca. And it was a story that he continued to play into over and over again. He felt deeply uncomfortable using his voice and speaking his truth. He found it excruciatingly difficult to share videos of himself with his online audience—videos which he felt were important to put out because it was a way for him to share his message and serve the people he knew he was here to serve.

Like me, Luca was raised in an Indian family that held certain views about who he needed to be to be accepted and loved by his family and his cultural society. He had been primed his entire life to please others and to show up in ways to not disappoint his family or lineage. This upbringing influenced Luca to play a role—to wear a false identity to receive the love and approval he desired. But that identity was diluting his potency. And by the time he started working with me, his false identity was so deeply ingrained that he struggled to be anything different—including himself.

Luca had developed a series of self-sabotaging behaviors, including perfectionism, avoidance, distraction, and self-deprecation. All of which would cause him to shut down and hide, even when he was desperately seeking to put himself out there and serve with intention.

Luca had been on a spiritual journey prior to working with me, and through that journey, he gained the ability to see many of the ways in which he was fucking himself up, but he continued to ignore what he saw in exchange for the comfort of what he had grown accustomed to: people-pleasing.

When Luca sent me that text, I took a moment to reflect on how I wanted to respond. On one hand, he knew why he was finding it so difficult to use his voice, speak, and be who he is. Yet, he was still choosing to deny what he saw and needed a reminder right then and there. So I responded with this:

"Better question . . . Why are you choosing NOT to challenge this?"

Luca knew that the only way through this was to stop playing into the same story by taking action to teach himself a new story—a new way of being. He knew this, but because of the extra effort involved in teaching himself a new behavior, he chose to hide behind his excuses and dilute his potency on purpose.

And we ALL do this.

It's far easier to live on autopilot and replay the same patterns and behaviors that fuel the same stories because we've grown accustomed to living this way. It's much more difficult to teach ourselves a new way—to respond differently, to show up differently, and to be different.

In that moment, Luca chose to take action to teach himself a new way of being. He recorded and shared his videos and despite feeling as if the videos weren't "good enough" or "perfect enough," he got the message out there and, in doing so, chose to create change. Luca chose to unleash his potency.

Does this mean that he no longer freezes with fear when it's time to share more videos or do something outside his comfort zone? No. But it means that he's now given himself an example of what's possible when he challenges his people-pleasing ways—an example that encourages him to continue to see and change all the ways in which he is fucking himself up.

Like Luca, you are diluting your potency on purpose. You want change. In fact, you crave it, yet you're unwilling to change. And that change can only happen when you choose to open your eyes to all the ways in which you're getting in your own damn way. It's time to own your shit.

CHAPTER 15:
WHAT ARE YOU AFRAID TO OWN?

> ▸ What parts of you are you most afraid to own? Think about it.
>
> ▸ What parts of you do you continue to ignore, brush under the rug, or dismiss? What are the parts of you that you continue to deny due to your fear of judgment or failure?
>
> ▸ What parts of you feel less than "perfect"?
>
> ▸ What parts of you are you ashamed or embarrassed by?
>
> ▸ What parts of you have you been told are not okay, too much, not enough, or unacceptable?

I dentify these parts of you. In fact, grab a journal and a pen and write this shit down. Because the quicker you let yourself see these parts of you, the quicker you'll be able to create change.

Identify your self-perceived faults, your fears, your false beliefs, and narratives. Dare to step inward and face your shadows. Because the answers you seek won't be found within the light—they're found within your shadows.

Welcome to your dark side. As in Star Wars, we all have dark and light within us. In fact, one cannot live without the other. This is the function of duality in our world. How would you know love if you didn't know hate? How would you know integrity if you didn't know deceit? How would you know your strengths if you didn't know your weaknesses? How would you know good if you didn't know bad? The truth is . . . you wouldn't. This is why duality exists. You cannot differentiate the darkness from everything else unless you have something to compare it with. This is why it's important for you to confront your shadows.

We've been trained to fear the dark, and that fear is keeping you from doing the real work—the inner-work. This unconscious and deeply embedded fear is causing you to avoid your darkness and bypass your shadows in favor of something better. But your perception of "better" has also been influenced by this narrative.

What if I were to tell you that there is no good or bad? That there is no light or dark? What if I were to tell you that the way in which we view anything is simply our perception, and that our perceptions are based on what we believe to be true?

What if I were to tell you that everything is neutral, and WE are the ones who give things a positive or negative charge?

That's the deep shit that I'm inviting you into. I'm inviting you into a deep exploration of self that will become your life-long journey—the journey of inner-work.

This journey consists of four phases that you will continuously cycle through:

Observation.

Reflection.

Transmutation.

Evolution.

THE PHASE OF OBSERVATION

This is about being aware enough to recognize the darkness within you, and courageous enough to uncover your shadows—no matter how scary, ugly, wrong, or bad they may feel.

THE PHASE OF REFLECTION

This is where you practice patience and self-compassion as you sit with all that you've uncovered, without judgement.

THE PHASE OF TRANSMUTATION

This is where you create change and shift your relationship with your shadows so you can start viewing them in a different light.

THE PHASE OF EVOLUTION

This is where you solidify your changes and practice integration, implementation, and improvement to embody this new iteration of self.

This is the work that you get to do—the work that is needed in order for you to unleash your potency. You must see all the ways in which you've been diluting yourself. You must walk with your shadows. In fact, I recommend that you keep your shadows in front of you so that they can't sneak up on you from behind. And you can do this by staying devoted to this journey.

Observe yourself, daily.

Reflect on what you observe, daily.

Transmute what needs to be changed, daily.

And take ownership of your evolution.

Piece by piece, you'll begin to chip away at the false identities that you've been wearing, uncovering more and more of you. Your habit of bypassing your shadows ends today, right here, right now.

If you're only preaching "love and light," you're missing the point. You are not all love and light. You are your shadows and your darkness and the gray areas in-between. This is the problem within the spiritual community; by focusing on "love and light" and "high vibes," you're missing out on experiencing all parts of you—the perceived good and the perceived bad. You're missing out on loving all parts of you, all of which holds you back from leading authentically and being in your potency.

It's crucial that you identify these parts of you—the parts that perhaps you've been denying or bypassing—because let's face it . . . it's easier to give in to the societal pressures and expectations of who you need to be versus just being you.

You can't be authentic if you're unwilling to walk within your dark side. Like everything in life, we experience duality within us, and that duality is yours to own. There are gifts within your dark side, but you won't see them if you continue denying those parts of you.

Think of it this way . . .

When you avoid seeing a certain aspect of yourself because you've been led to believe that it's wrong or bad or not acceptable, you avoid seeing yourself. And when you don't see yourself, how can you expect others to really see you? This is why you don't feel seen.

Being a Potent Leader isn't about perfection—it's about being so fucking self-aware that you're able to show up while embracing your shadows and your darkness. It's about doing the inner-work while you're in the spotlight, and not feeling like you have to hide until you are "perfect" or bypass the inner-work altogether because you're in a rush to be seen as a leader.

The truth that no one is telling you is that the path of Potent Leadership is messy as fuck. It's messy because you dare to be seen as you are, without posturing, editing, or filtering yourself. It's about being honest about what you don't know, and being real about who you are. All of that begins with you having the courage to walk the dark side of yourself so you can see all parts of who you be. And once you gain the ability to see yourself, you get to do the inner-work to own who you be—the work that you've been bypassing for far too long.

At some point in your life, you were shown that it's unsafe to own your shadows. Whether it was when you were five years old and you denied hitting your younger sibling because your mom was threatening to punish you, or you were fourteen years old and you denied sneaking out of the house because your dad was pissed and threatening to ground you, you learned that in order to keep yourself feeling safe, you'd sometimes need to lie or hide your shadows.

Now, this behavior has become so entrenched in your being that you fail to recognize that you do this. But self-preservation is built into your system, and many of the things that you're doing to keep yourself feeling safe is actually keeping you from dropping into your potency.

→ Maybe you're claiming to have skills that you don't have because you're scared of being seen as an imposter.
→ Maybe you're pretending to be someone you're not, in fear of being judged or hated for who you are.
→ Maybe you're quick to delete content or deny what you said when you realize that you're wrong because you're so desperate to be seen as an expert.

You're holding yourself back from creating the changes you seek by refusing to see all the ways in which you're getting in your own damn way. This self-preservation is keeping you from owning your shit and experiencing the freedom of being who you are.

At some point in your life, hiding, lying, playing small, pretending, posturing, filtering, and editing yourself kept you safe. It served a purpose. But now, it's holding you back.

The moment you own your shadows is the moment you gain the power to create change.

All the changes you seek can only happen when you are willing to take responsibility for your life. Now this may sound like basic personal development, but I can guarantee that you're still not willing to own all your shadows. If you're struggling to unleash your potency, it's because you're ignoring all the ways in which you're diluting it.

When you own your shadows, you start to break down the dissonance within you—the dissonance that you've created. This creates an opening for you to uncover more of who you be, while letting go of the parts of you that aren't really you. This is where the cycle of inner-work is needed. To observe who you be, to reflect on what you discover, uncover, and let go of, to transmute what needs to be changed, and to take charge of your evolution through integration, implementation, and improvement.

Owning your shadows is truly the first step to embodying your potency, and it's the step that many leaders bypass because they're in such a rush to be seen as a leader. But how can you expect to be a leader if you're not BEING a leader?

I know by now, at this stage in your evolution, you've heard of the importance of embodiment. But do you truly understand what it means? Do you truly understand how you and your leadership would shift if you embodied your potency?

When it comes to who you be, embodiment is the act of expressing, personifying, or exemplifying all that you are.

You have to live it, breathe it, and BE who you be, and not just pretend to be. You must be the fullest expression of everything you teach, preach, and share. You must be a living example of your message, your mission, and your movement. So much so that you no longer feel the need to prove yourself to others. This is what it means to embody your potency.

Owning your shadows is the first step to embodying your potency, and it's a step that you'll find yourself taking over and over again because as you continue to evolve, there's always going to be new shadows for you to own.

> ▸ What shadows are you ready to own?
>
> ▸ And how will things shift once you fully own your shadows?

CHAPTER 16:
WHAT DO YOU BELIEVE?

Have you ever stopped to question whether your beliefs are really yours?

Now is that time. I'm inviting you to question the beliefs that you're carrying.

- ▶ What are your beliefs around **success**?
- ▶ What are your beliefs around **money**?
- ▶ What are your beliefs around **confidence**?
- ▶ What are your beliefs around **freedom**?
- ▶ What are your beliefs around **authority**?
- ▶ What are your beliefs around **worthiness**?
- ▶ What are your beliefs around **leadership**?
- ▶ What are your beliefs around **being seen**?
- ▶ What are your beliefs around **speaking up**?
- ▶ What are your beliefs around **authenticity**?

The list goes on. I'm inviting you to question everything, because I guarantee you that many of your beliefs are not your beliefs—they're false beliefs projected upon you by your parents, your culture, your religion, your experiences, and society. By identifying the false beliefs, you'll gain the insight to uncover what you truly believe—your chosen beliefs.

Your beliefs influence your choices, your decisions, and your actions. But these beliefs are embedded in your unconscious mind—the part of your mind that is constantly running in the background without your awareness. And since your beliefs have such a massive influence on you, it's easy to run on autopilot, eventually finding yourself living a life that doesn't feel like yours, designing a business that doesn't feel right, and showing up in ways that just don't feel aligned.

You have within you a set of false beliefs, and if you don't identify what these beliefs are, you'll continue to fall victim to them. If you find yourself moving in a direction that doesn't feel right or aligned, question your beliefs.

I used to believe that success was based on the size of my house, the number and types of cars in my driveway, how much money I made, and the type of lifestyle I lived. And I used to believe that I had to work hard and sacrifice to be successful. I believed this because this is what I witnessed within my household growing up. But this version of success was part of my dad's story, not mine.

Being raised in India, my dad was immersed in our Indian culture where money and status mattered. This is a culture where dowries are exchanged at weddings and caste systems determine the direction of your future. So what you had mattered. My grandfather worked hard to build up our family name. At one point, he even left his family behind to pursue business opportunities in Africa, sacrificing time with his family because this was seen as a sacrifice FOR the family. Eventually, my grandfather built a successful business and moved the family to the UK, establishing roots there. This is what my dad witnessed growing up: sacrifices and working hard, all in the pursuit of our culture's version of success, which translates to status and having the means to take care of your family.

My grandfather was hard on my dad—he expected a lot of his kids. He also projected his beliefs upon them, leading them (my dad included) to adopt the same beliefs as him. And this is how the cycle of our belief systems is repeated. They're passed down through our lineage—generations of the same cycles repeated until one brave soul chooses to question what they believe.

My dad works harder than anyone I know. He modeled hard work, passion, and drive for me. He also projected his beliefs on success onto my siblings and me—the beliefs that were projected onto him: work hard and create status. And because I believed his story of success, I began hustling hard and chasing the same things.

For a long time, I wanted the big house and the fancy cars. At one point in my twenties, I was working at a financial institution and a retail store, while also running a makeup artistry and esthetics business—working all day, seven days a week, and saving tons of money without really even understanding why I was hustling so hard. This "work hard and create status" belief stayed with me until my thirties, influencing all of my choices, decisions, and actions, leading me to design a life that did not feel like my own. But when I hit rock bottom and started questioning everything, I realized that this life was not what I wanted and that my beliefs on success are far different. I realized that I had been chasing the wrong things due to a false belief.

I realized that I'm a damn good hustler, but hustling and working hard was making me sick. So instead, I chose to believe that success requires energy and intention.

I realized that while I do appreciate the finer things in life, I'm happier barefoot on the earth, hugging trees, and spending time with the people I love.

I realized that status does matter in our world (unfortunately), but that there are also ways to create a sense of status without playing a game of show and tell, by focusing on who I'm being in this world.

Today, I believe that success is about how I feel at the end of each day: having the freedom to be who I am, surrounding myself with people I love, having the ability to give back to myself and others in different ways, being present and grateful for every moment, creating more time for myself and family, and living a healthy lifestyle that feels good by my standards. This is my CHOSEN belief about success, and it's the belief that drives my current choices, decisions, and actions.

You have within you a set of false beliefs that are influencing who you're being, and the life that you're creating. These beliefs may have been passed down through generations in your lineage or they may have been something you picked up through society and your experiences. Either way, it's up to you to dismantle these false beliefs while you identify your chosen beliefs—the beliefs that you truly wish to believe because these are the beliefs that will help you amplify your potency and be the leader you're here to be.

> ▶ What are your false beliefs around **success**?
> And what do you choose to believe instead?
>
> ▶ What are your false beliefs around **money**?
> And what do you choose to believe instead?
>
> ▶ What are your false beliefs around **confidence**?
> And what do you choose to believe instead?
>
> ▶ What are your false beliefs around **freedom**?
> And what do you choose to believe instead?
>
> ▶ What are your false beliefs around **authority**?
> And what do you choose to believe instead?
>
> ▶ What are your false beliefs around **worthiness**?
> And what do you choose to believe instead?

- ▶ What are your false beliefs around **leadership**? And what do you choose to believe instead?

- ▶ What are your false beliefs around **being seen**? And what do you choose to believe instead?

- ▶ What are your false beliefs around **speaking up**? And what do you choose to believe instead?

- ▶ What are your false beliefs around **authenticity**? And what do you choose to believe instead?

CHAPTER 17:

WHAT ARE YOUR NON-NEGOTIABLES?

Do you know what you value? What's *really* important to you?

Sounds like a simple question, but from working with leaders one on one, in leading my group programs, or in hosting my events, this question always seems to stump the person I ask.

Every single leader I've worked with assumes that they know what they value, but after diving deeper with me, they end up identifying a different set of values than they thought—*these* are their real values. Or as I prefer to call them, your non-negotiables.

Your non-negotiables are the foundation for who you be, as well as everything you build and create—they become the blueprint for you to design a life, business, and movement that feels really fucking good. Your non-negotiables help you stay in alignment with your potent self.

The real reason you're experiencing a lack of alignment in your life is that you've been abiding by a set of FALSE non-negotiables—saying yes to things that aren't truly aligned while overlooking opportunities for true alignment, which leads to a dilution of your potency.

Have you ever heard yourself say things like . . .

"This just doesn't feel right."

"Something's off."

"This doesn't feel good."

Or perhaps you continue to feel energetically depleted, unfulfilled, and like you're sacrificing something but you can't quite place your finger on what it is that you're sacrificing.

These are all signs that you're not honoring the things that are truly most important to you—your non-negotiables. And to be fair, you were never encouraged to uncover your own set of non-negotiables, but you were taught to value what your family or society deems as important— you learned to adopt a set of false non-negotiables.

Most people negotiate their non-negotiables.

And yes, this includes you. Similar to your beliefs, your non-negotiables influence who you're being and the life that you're creating. They are your blueprint, so if you're following the wrong blueprint, you'll end up building something that doesn't feel good or right or aligned. Running on autopilot with a false set of non-negotiables will influence you to make choices and decisions that lead to outcomes that you don't really desire.

Think about it. . .

> ▶ Have you ever achieved a goal only to be left feeling unfulfilled? Questioning why you're feeling what you're feeling and wondering why the experience felt so incredibly anticlimactic?

It's because you're chasing the wrong things.

You have yet to identify what's really important to you, and you're negotiating your non-negotiables—all of which is diluting your potency and making you less of who you truly are.

This is the reason why I see many leaders burnt out and frustrated from chasing the idea of "scaling" their business. I've worked with multiple leaders who have struggled to create large membership platforms and sell digital courses as an attempt to "10x" their business. And by taking the time to dive deeper into this with them, we uncover that they're negotiating a lot to chase what they think they want without ever questioning if it's what they really want.

Some leaders truly want to scale their business with thousands of clients, millions in sales, all while building a large team of support around them. And then there are leaders (like myself and many people that I've served) who value intimacy, depth, and connection. Neither is better than the other, but as you can probably tell, they have different outcomes. One outcome could be a business with low-cost, one-to-many offers, and the other outcome could be a business with high-end, intimate groups and services. And again, neither is better than the other. But if you're chasing the wrong things and negotiating your true non-negotiables, the outcomes that you create will not be aligned—they won't feel good or right or fulfilling.

You have to stop placing importance on what others deem as important.

You have to stop living your life according to another person's desires or expectations.

You have to stop leading your life for "them" and start leading it for you. The outcomes that you desire can only be created when you follow your inner-blueprint. You need to create an internal shift to experience an external shift, and you can only do that by asking yourself the right questions.

It's time for you to audit your life.

- ▶ What's REALLY important to you?
- ▶ What REALLY matters to you?
- ▶ What feels meaningful to you?
- ▶ **What are your non-negotiables?**

CHAPTER 18:
ARE YOU DEVOTED?

Devotion runs deeper than discipline and takes you further than commitment. And yet society has you believing otherwise . . .

Society wants you to believe that discipline and commitment are needed to achieve your goals. They want you to believe that discipline and commitment are needed to pursue your purpose. They want you to believe that discipline and commitment are needed to be the leader you know you're here to be.

But discipline and commitment are not the answer. The answer is devotion.

When you think of disciplining yourself to achieve something or become something, how does that feel in your body? Does it feel rigid? Controlled? Forced?

When you're training yourself to do something or become something in a controlled and habitual way (i.e., with discipline), you're taking your heart out of what you're doing and who you're being. You're pushing yourself to make something happen for the sake of making it happen. You may even be forcing yourself to make something happen due to the fear of not making it happen.

And I get it. The personal development industry pushes the idea of discipline down our throats.

Does discipline work? Yes.

But does discipline FEEL good? Only when it's ignited from a state of devotion. Discipline is the container for devotion. And that's where most people miss the mark. They lack devotion. When it comes to commitment, it's crucial that you only commit to things that feel right and aligned with you. Devotion guides you in creating commitments that support your potency.

If you truly want to be a Potent Leader, devotion is needed.

Devotion is what happens when passion and purpose meet dedication. It's about finding something you're passionate about—something that feels purposeful and meaningful to you. When you become devoted to doing something or becoming something, you'll feel an emotional pull to make it happen because it means something to you.

Being devoted to your purpose, your vision, and yourself is about finding true loyalty and love for the outcomes that you desire. It's about leading with heart, not fear. It's about following what feels right for you—the things that will ignite your potency.

Devotion cultivates a sense of discipline that feels exciting, not controlled, and it helps you understand what you really want to commit to doing and who you truly want to commit to being. This devotion must start within.

It's easy to devote yourself to serving others, or to devote yourself to your business or your clients. What's tough is being devoted to yourself. I know this firsthand.

In my culture, we're raised to respect our elders, abide by their rules, and fulfill their expectations. We're taught to selflessly serve others through "seva," a major component of our religion. Women especially are trained to put their needs second to the needs of others in the family. But never was I ever taught to serve myself. In fact, I'd be labeled selfish anytime I made that attempt. And this is something that is found in all cultures.

The spiritual and personal development communities are very much the same, preaching that the quickest way to feel better is to serve others. Although this has some truth to it, this type of belief also encourages you to sweep your feelings under the rug while experiencing the temporary high that comes with serving others. This is simply a Band-Aid effect. The shit you're feeling inside will always be there until you deal with it. And that can only happen when you make your own personal and spiritual growth a priority.

Leadership is an inner-game. This isn't about how many people you serve—it's about the depth of your service. Since you can only go as deep with others as you've gone within yourself, it's important that you create a devotion to self.

Up until my early thirties, I was living my life for others. Devoting myself to pleasing others, to being like "them," to fitting in and being accepted. I brought this behavior into my business. Within three years, I was burnt out, physically and energetically depleted, and emotionally drained; the worst part was that I started to resent my work and my clients.

I was battling severe anxiety, experiencing regular anxiety attacks in the middle of the night, having mysterious waves of deep depression and suicidal thoughts, and having major gut-health issues. I could barely focus and get work done, and I realized that something had to give. I had had enough. I knew there had to be a better way . . . I just needed to find it. At the end of 2018, I made the conscious decision to become devoted to myself and my healing—I chose to devote myself to the inner-work.

I stopped enrolling clients. I stopped promoting and marketing my services. Except for the clients I already worked with, I closed the doors on my business so I could face what I was dealing with head-on.

Trust me, it isn't an easy decision to shut your business down as an entrepreneur. My head was filled with "what if's."

What if I run out of money?

What if my business goes under?

What if I become irrelevant?

What if I miss out on big opportunities?

But another question arose . . .

Is any of this really worth losing myself, my health, and my well-being?

No. After all, there is no business and no movement without me. I am the foundation for everything that I'm building. The inner-work is mandatory.

I had no idea where that path would lead me, but I'm so grateful that I had the courage to create a devotion to self. Because today, I'm happy and fulfilled, I love my business, and I have extremely healthy and loving boundaries with myself, my business, my social media, and my clients.

My devotion to self is the reason I've completely redesigned my business. It's the reason why I'm able to attract aligned AF clients and an incredible community with ease. By being devoted to myself, I've gained the ability to create success by being the fullest expression of who I am—my potent self. Because each and every single day, I'm choosing to honor my growth, my evolution, and my healing by staying devoted to the inner-work.

So let me ask you this . . .

And finally, moving forward . . .

When it comes to your success as a leader, don't force it through discipline alone. BECOME a successful and Potent Leader through devotion.

Be devoted to your purpose.

Be devoted to your vision.

Be devoted to all that is meaningful to you.

And above all else, be devoted to yourself. Because nothing else matters if you're not devoted to who you're being.

CHAPTER 19:
DO YOU TRUST YOURSELF?

Your never-ending chase for perfection, your people-pleasing ways, your habit of filtering yourself in public . . .

These are all symptoms of a lack of self-trust.

While this may seem like a surprise . . . hear me out, because I've been exactly where you are.

I've spent way too much of my life trying to perfect everything, including my image, my social media posts, and my events, offers, and programs. I lived a large portion of my life for others, pleasing them and trying to gain their love and acceptance. I've spent years filtering my physical self in every way imaginable. I used to think that this behavior was due to my fear of judgment, my fear of not being enough, or my fear of being unloved . . . but this ran so much deeper than that.

After decades of living life trying to please my family and abide by our cultural expectations while not being true to myself, I developed a profound fear of judgment and an incredibly crippling fear of being unloved. I started to lose sight of who I was and what I truly wanted. It wasn't until my journey back from rock bottom in 2012 that I started to heal these fears and my worthiness wounds. What I didn't know was that there was something much deeper at play, but it took me going into the Amazon jungle to uncover what it was. What happened there forever changed my life because that's where I learned self-trust.

It was November 2019, and I had just arrived in a small village called Pahoyan in the Amazon jungle of Peru. The village (like many other villages in the Amazon) is situated along the Ucayali River, and we traveled four and a half hours by river boat to get there. I was in Pahoyan to sit in plant medicine dieta for fourteen days with the renowned Shipibo healer, Papa Gilberto Mahua.

This was the first time I had done anything like this. I had drank the psychedelic plant medicine, *ayahuasca,* many times before—in fact, I was deep in the midst of a healing journey with plant medicine that had begun ten months prior—but this was different: traveling solo to a foreign country, living in the jungle with the bare minimum, going on a fourteen-day dieta, abstaining from sex, digital devices, media, on a strict diet that had me eating plain mushy food, and not knowing what to expect. The "control freak" in me was being challenged.

I remember seeing my *tambo* for the first time—a bare-bones bamboo hut built on four stilts with a thatched roof and netting as windows. I walked inside, took a deep breath, and thought to myself, "How the fuck am I going to do this?" I was sharing this tambo with another woman—someone I had just met. This would be her second time in Pahoyan this year, so she seemed quite comfortable and elated to be there.

I, on the other hand, was not. The tambo was barren except for two small wooden desks, two small wooden benches, and the dirtiest, moldiest single mattress I had ever seen. I soon found out that that mattress was my bed and felt immediately grateful for the mattress protector that I had packed due to a recommendation from a friend.

Looking around the tambo I quickly noticed that the mosquito netted windows and ceiling did not keep all the bugs out. In fact, the entire tambo was crawling with bugs and spiders that were literally the size of my hand. There was one light bulb hanging high up from the center of the thatched roof, and one outlet. The entire village had electricity, but only between the hours of 6:00 p.m. and 9:00 p.m. each night. Later, I found out that having the light on meant attracting all the bugs to our tambo, so we left the light off.

I took a tour of the village and saw the *maloca* (our ceremony space), the two toilets and two showers powered by rainwater, the bath house, the rickety wooden outhouses (which looked absolutely terrifying), and the kitchen and the dining area where we would eat our dieta-friendly meals.

I was completely out of my comfort zone. Now don't get me wrong. I have been traveling around the world since I was five years old. I had been to India over six times, lived in Mumbai for ten months in my early twenties, walked the border between Punjab and Pakistan to visit a historic Sikh temple in Hasan Abdal, traveled throughout China (walking the Great Wall and doing humanitarian work in a small village near Guangzhou), and traveled through other countries such as Thailand, Singapore, and Bali. Travel was always deeply valued by my parents because they did not want their kids to take our lives in Canada (where I was raised) for granted.

That said, again, I was completely out of my comfort zone. Although I was there with a small group of people, I only knew two of those people intimately prior to being in Peru. I missed my husband, Kevin, deeply and had no idea how I was going to go an entire fourteen days without being in contact with him. And that was part of my intention—to gain back a feeling of independence (or so I thought . . . keep reading).

We were in Pahoyan to specifically work with Papa Gilberto Mahua on what's called a master plant dieta. A master plant dieta is a highly disciplined process that involves dieting a *planta maestra* (teacher plant) or *plantas que enseñan* (plants and trees that teach) to transmit guidance, protection, and sacred knowledge to the *dietero* (the student). In addition to the master plants and trees, you're also fasting from many types of food, abstaining from sex, and limiting your interactions and engagement with other people as well as limiting the information that you're taking in (i.e., books, music, etc.).

I was specifically prescribed a diet with *bobinsana* and *noya rao*, which I would drink as teas in addition to sitting with ayahuasca, and we would sit in ceremony with "aya" every other night that we were there, six times total in a span of fourteen days. Since I had only sat with ayahuasca seven times prior in the comforts of California, I had no idea what to expect in the jungles of Peru. All I knew was that I had been called there for a reason.

Going to Peru wasn't a random decision. Since January 2019, after sitting with ayahuasca only once, I knew that I would find myself in Peru in November. I didn't know how, but I knew it would happen. I saw it in a vision. Fast forward to November, and I was there. Everything lined up to make this happen. I was able to pause all my client calls for a month with my clients' blessings, pause my business, and create space in my schedule to leave everything behind for this trip.

The ayahuasca ceremonies were intense and like nothing I had ever imagined. One night blurred into the next night, and I experienced an entire deconstruction of my mind and body. What I want to make super clear here is that when you sit with this type of medicine, you cannot go with an expectation, only intentions. And my intentions were to work through my traumas, gain clarity, and learn more about myself. You also need to understand that sitting with these medicines won't always provide you with an incredible psychedelic experience. In fact, most of my ceremonies in the jungle were filled with immense physical and emotional pain. I was facing my shadows, seeing all the ways in which I was getting in my own way, and gaining the ability to truly see my ancestral trauma and how that trauma has impacted my life.

I remember one night specifically. It was our third night sitting with ayahuasca and I was struggling—really struggling. I was angry at myself for not purging, upset at myself for getting it wrong, frustrated with myself for the anger I felt, and deeply saddened at the fact that I was being so hard on myself in that ceremony. Eyes closed, crouched down on my mat, shoving my fingers down my throat trying to force myself to purge into my bucket, sobbing . . . I heard myself cry for help, which is something that I've always struggled to do, due to my fear of rejection. When I finally opened my eyes to see my guide, Robin, and friends surrounding me, chanting *Shipibo icaros* (prayers) to me, holding space for me while in their own ceremonies. The tears came down even harder, seeing for the first time just how supported I truly was. Robin (who has also now become a dear brother of mine) escorted me outside for some fresh air underneath the starlit sky. I hung on to his arm as he slowly walked me out of the maloca. As soon as we got outside, I took a deep breath. I leaned over the rail of the bridge just outside the maloca and continued to force myself to purge. Screaming, crying, and in so much physical pain, I could barely stand.

"I can't purge!" I told him. "I'm forcing myself to purge but it's not coming out!"

That's when he said, "What would happen if you stopped forcing things to happen?"

"But it hurts!" I said. I was in so much pain. My gut felt like it was being twisted and torn apart, and I assumed that by purging, I would release that pain.

"And what would happen if you sat with that pain?" he asked.

That's when I stopped for a minute, barely standing, hanging onto the wooden rail. I looked up and saw the overwhelming beauty in the night sky. The black sky was the darkest I had ever seen, and the stars were the brightest I had ever seen. I felt the pain, and I let myself feel the pain. In that moment, I trusted myself enough to be with the pain, all without trying to bypass it or fix it or push my way through it. And eventually, the pain passed. There wasn't anything that I needed to do or control to get through that pain—I simply had to be with it and trust myself enough to be with it.

I learned many life-changing lessons during my first dieta, and more lessons continue to come to the surface because that experience was just the beginning of the deconstruction and reconstruction process. But one lesson stood out, and that was **self-trust.**

If I had gone to the jungle and not partaken in a plant medicine dieta, I still would have felt just as challenged. The environment alone shook me. With the dense, thick darkness of night that made it tough to see one foot in front of you, the spiders the size of my hands, the rattlesnakes rattling outside my tambo, the surplus of bugs that left bite marks all over my body, the monsoon rains that flooded the village floor, the rain boots that seemed to always be filled with cockroaches, the intense heat and humidity that left all my clothes feeling wet all the time, the moldy single mattress that I slept on, the bucket next to my mattress that I used as a nightly bathroom, and the overwhelming sounds of the jungle . . . . I felt challenged in every way imaginable. I was being challenged to trust myself.

What became apparent to me in Pahoyan was how much I did not trust myself. Remember when I mentioned that one of my intentions was to regain my independence? What I realized was that this went way deeper than that.

I didn't trust myself enough to walk alone at night during my first few nights there—I felt unsafe.

I didn't trust myself enough to feel loved by others without my makeup, clean hair, and clean clothes—to feel accepted in my bare skin.

I didn't trust myself enough to really let go and surrender in a few ceremonies, and I was immediately met with the pain of not letting go in physical form.

I didn't trust myself enough to be on my own with no distractions. I felt uncomfortable with the voices in my head.

I didn't trust myself, and the jungle was gifting me the ability to see all the ways in which my lack of self-trust was impacting me and my life.

I had been living with the symptoms of a lack of self-trust my entire life and didn't even know it: my perfectionist ways, my need to control, my desire to know the exact plan, and my false identity that had me posturing, editing, and filtering myself in life and in business.

I did not trust myself. And once I gained the ability to see this lack of self-trust, I saw it in everything that I was doing and all the versions of myself that I was being.

I came back from Peru without my false identity, and I haven't worn that false identity since. I've never felt more free, more confident, more potent, or more me. When I started working again, I set the intention to work with fewer, but more deeply aligned, clients in 2020. I decided that I would fill my coaching programs for that year by February 2020 so I could continue to nurture the spaciousness and lessons that I learned from Peru throughout the following year. I was determined to do things differently, because I was different. I now trust myself.

I filled my coaching programs by February with the most aligned AF clients I had ever been honored to work with, and I owe it all to the fact that I trusted myself enough to no longer wear a false identity.

No more posturing as an attempt to control how I am perceived . . . because I trust myself.

No more editing myself to please my audience and impress my peers . . . because I trust who I am.

No more filtering myself because I don't feel worthy enough to be seen as me . . . because I trust who I'm being.

The false identity is gone. And the same gets to happen for you.

You have to trust yourself enough to show up and lead your purpose as you. No posturing, no editing, no filtering. Just you, being the fullest expression of who you are. After all, this is YOUR purpose, and it's meant to be led and fulfilled by you.

Unlike what many people believe, your purpose was not gifted to you—it was birthed by you. It was created through your experiences and alchemized through your traumas, your wounds, and your story. You created your purpose, which means that it needs you to lead it. The false identity that you've created to keep yourself safe no longer works. It served its purpose, but now, it's time to rediscover who you be.

All the effort that you've been using to try and control how you're being perceived (the sacrifices that you've made to please and impress others and the energy that it takes to filter yourself all the time), *is it really worth it?* What are you really gaining by wearing a false identity? When you were younger, the posturing, editing, and filtering yourself kept you feeling safe, loved, and accepted by those around you. But what about now?

You don't have to go to the Amazon jungle to see all the ways in which this behavior is no longer serving you. All you must do is ask yourself these questions:

> - Am I attracting the right people into my business and movement?
> - Am I attracting opportunities that feel aligned with what I really want?
> - Am I only saying "yes" to people, things, and experiences that feel good to me?
> - Am I doing what I want to do?
> - Am I BEING who I want to be?

If you answered no to any or all these questions, you don't trust yourself. And this is why you continue to dilute your potency by depending on your false identity. The only reason you don't trust yourself is because you experienced something to sabotage that trust. Whether you were rejected, abandoned, shamed, judged, ridiculed, or punished for being you, that experience became embedded in your unconscious mind and transformed into a belief that you continue to believe.

"I'm too much for others."

"People never take me seriously."

"People always judge me."

"I'm never accepted by others when I'm being me."

"Every time I'm honest with people, they leave."

"I need to show up in a certain way in order to feel loved and accepted by others."

"I don't trust myself."

Whatever the belief, it's a belief that is fueling your posturing, editing, and filtering behavior; it's causing you to dilute your potency, and all these beliefs boil down to a lack of self-trust.

You might think that you don't trust other people, or certain environments (like me in Pahoyan) or experiences, but the truth is, you don't trust yourself.

SELF-TRUST

LACK OF SELF-TRUST

SELF-TRUST	LACK OF SELF-TRUST
Understands their worth	Chases perfection
Shows up as a leader	Shows up as a people-pleaser
Authentic	Wears masks
Speaks their truth	Filters themselves
Stands with conviction	Filled with self-doubt
Values self	Engages in self-sabotage
Confident	Insecure
Feels certain about who they are	Always feels uncertain

Just as you sabotaged your own sense of self-trust, you also get to rebuild it. How? By allowing yourself the opportunity to do so. If you continue to posture, edit, and filter yourself, you'll never allow yourself the *opportunity* to build self-trust. Just as I did in the jungle by immersing myself in an environment where I was forced to trust myself, you get to create a similar opportunity, and you don't need the jungle to make that happen.

Our minds are interesting and complex and also paradoxically simple. When you are searching for something specific, you'll see it everywhere, while dismissing anything different. Here's an experiment you can try that will show you how this works. The next time you're driving or taking transit, focus on finding all the red cars on the road (or whichever color you choose). You will start to notice all the red cars, and you'll start to notice just how many red cars there are. At the same time, you'll pay no attention to how many other different colored cars there are on the road. Your brain works the same way.

You are constantly seeking out evidence to validate your beliefs. Your unconscious mind is perpetually attuned to what you focus on.

> ▶ If your current belief is that you don't trust yourself, what would happen if you started to tell yourself that you do trust yourself?
>
> ▶ What would happen if you started to give yourself opportunities to trust yourself?
>
> ▶ What would happen if you stopped posturing as an attempt to control how you're being perceived and just let yourself be you?
>
> ▶ What would happen if you stopped editing yourself to please those around you and just let yourself be you?

> ▶ What would happen if you stopped filtering yourself and just let yourself be you?

I'll tell you what would happen. You'd put yourself in a situation where you get to cultivate self-trust and self-worth.

CHAPTER 20:
WHAT'S YOUR LEGACY?

Most leaders bypass the inner-work because they're fixated on instant "likes," instant "follows," instant sales, and instant ROI. They're obsessed with how they're perceived, and they prioritize image over integrity. What they don't realize is that they're sacrificing their potency for their ego, all while presenting a diluted version of themselves to the world. Most leaders rush to experience immediate results. But you need to understand this:

Leadership is not a short-term game— it's about creating a lasting legacy.

I'll admit, there's a certain glorification that comes with attending business seminars that promise you immediate sales and scalability, or working with business coaches that promise you higher income months so you can travel the world and work from your laptop. But if you're not being who you need to be to execute, take action, or build something with longevity that actually feels aligned with you, then what's the fucking point?

I have worked with countless leaders who come to me after having completed multiple courses and worked with business coaches, claiming that they're still not where they want to be. They feel overworked, overwhelmed, and unfulfilled. They feel as if they've done everything but have nothing to show for it, and they're ready to do things differently. So, I introduce them to the inner-work. I guide them inward so they can shift their focus from what they're doing to who they're being. I support them in cultivating a devotion to themselves so they can start building a life and business that aligns with their chosen beliefs and true values—a life and business that leave a legacy.

Everything that you're seeking will only be found within you. Everything. In fact, your life is your legacy. Who you're being is what people will remember, not what you're doing or how many followers you've accumulated. Do you really think people will remember you for your social media fame? Do you really believe that your level of popularity matters to people? No. None of that shit means anything after you're gone. What matters is who you're being.

Work to build a legacy, not likes. Create a life of meaning—a life where you get to express yourself fully. That is the only way you'll leave an imprint on the hearts of others.

→   Show up and be of service.
→   Pursue things to fulfill your purpose.
→   Be devoted to yourself.
→   Embrace your potency.

THIS IS YOUR LEGACY.

"Please think about your legacy, because you're writing it every day."

—Gary Vaynerchuk[8]

In a world where we've become addicted to instant gratification, it's important to remember that leadership isn't instant—it's a journey, and that journey, not the destination, becomes your legacy.

You won't create a legacy if you're not focused on who you're being. You won't experience freedom if you don't feel free. You won't experience abundance if you don't feel abundant. And the confidence that you're chasing can only be found within you. This is an inner-game. So instead of letting your ego lead the way, be brave enough to dive inward and devote yourself to a life of legacy.

Be brave enough to swap your need for instant gratification for a journey that will support you in being you—a journey that will help you be the Potent Leader you're here to be so you can lead with integrity, be the fullest expression of who you are, and stand with conviction in your gifts, your presence, and your voice.

"You make your mark by being true to who you are and letting that be your staple."

—Kat Graham[9]

Your potency is your medicine, your legacy, and a gift that you get to offer yourself and the world. Your potency is how you'll be remembered. It's who you BE.

While your legacy might be made minute by minute, I'm inviting you to think beyond the immediate moment—to think beyond what you accomplish today and focus instead on who you're being. I invite

---

8. "Barry Vaynerchuck Quotes," AZ Quotes, https://www.azquotes.com/quote/521004.
9. "Kat Graham Quotes," BrainyQuote.com, accessed April 7, 2021, https://www.brainyquote.com/quotes/kat_graham_638961.

you to think about the impact you have on those around you because no matter how you're showing up, you're leaving an impact.

This brings me to the argument of impact versus intention, which always reminds me of the chicken versus the egg—what comes first?

You may have the greatest intentions in the world, but your impact could leave people feeling not so great. As a leader, it's your responsibility to understand the effect of your impact because your impact becomes your legacy. This isn't about people-pleasing or conforming—this is about heightening your awareness to ensure that your thoughts and actions are aligned with your intentions. It's about awareness of who you're being at all times.

Some people will judge you, hate you, and feel rubbed the wrong way by you. That's just evidence that you're being true to yourself and not trying to make everyone happy. Your potency isn't for everyone, and it's not meant to be. But being aware and understanding of your impact is your responsibility. Be who you be, and pay attention to the impact you're having on people who are aligned with you. Your potency is your legacy.

One of the ways we increase our potency is through mastery. Have you ever stopped to consider that the journey of mastery is one that never ends? Since everything in our world is constantly changing and evolving, how can we ever really "master" anything?

This includes mastery of self.

I remember saying to my former coach in one of our sessions, "I want to master coaching."

He looked at me for a moment, tilted his head, and replied with, "And when you master coaching, then what?"

"Well, then I'd be a master coach," I said.

To which he replied, "To master something means that there's nothing left to learn."

I sat silent for a few minutes, contemplating what he just said. The concept of mastery as a journey versus an end goal was new to me, but it made sense. Even knives get dull and need to be sharpened from time to time. What if mastery was really a journey with no end? A journey where I continue to sharpen my tools and be better with each passing day? This is self-mastery.

From my experience, self-mastery is a practice that involves two things: awareness and adaptability.

Have the awareness to observe yourself, your thoughts, and your actions. Have the adaptability to change, shift, transmute, or transform yourself, your thoughts, and your actions. Together, these two things create the practice of self-mastery—a practice that can only be found in the inner-work.

Self-mastery is about getting back into your habit of waking up early and working out after falling off-track. It's about having the resilience to get back up when you fail. It's about being devoted to doing your best and being your best each and every single day.

Because you will fall. You will fail. You will be knocked down. You will be thrown off your game. You will fuck up. This is inevitable. But what matters is what you do and who you choose to be in those moments. This is what self-mastery means—to focus on being and doing your absolute best, no matter what. Self-mastery is a journey within itself, but it's also the journey toward your legacy. As you continue to expand your awareness and practice adaptability—as you continue to understand the impact that you have on others—you also begin to create your legacy.

Like I said, leadership is not a short-term game—it's about creating a lasting legacy. And this legacy reflects who you be.

> ▶ How do you want to be remembered?
> ▶ How do you want people to describe your legacy?

CHAPTER 21:

ARE YOU WORTHY?

It's easy to hide on social media. In fact, social media is built to support you in hiding who you are. Think about it . . . the filters, the ability to edit what you share, and the ability to literally state who you are and what you're about in your bio and on your website. You get to be whoever you want to be and that presents an issue. If deep down inside, you don't feel worthy, that lack of self-worth will influence you to create what you think is a likable persona because you believe that this persona will gain the validation you seek through your audience.

Whether you're aware of it or not, you are hiding pieces of yourself from your audience because you don't feel worthy. You are also positioning yourself as something you're not because you don't feel worthy enough as the person you are.

Your battle with self-worth is like a cut that never heals because you continue to cover it up with Band-Aids. You're afraid to look at it because you're afraid of what that will mean about you.

How can I serve others if I don't feel worthy of my gifts?

How can I attract clients if I don't feel worthy of their business?

How can I build a business if I don't feel worthy of my prices?

How can I be successful if I don't feel worthy of success?

How can I be a leader if I don't feel worthy?

These questions are just some of the things that you find yourself ruminating on, and at times, these thoughts seem to take over your world.

Your worthiness issue is diluting your potency and keeping you in hiding. You're not being the leader you know you're here to be because deep down inside, you don't feel worthy.

Your battle with self-worth started years ago—perhaps even decades ago. Your worthiness issue may run so deep, you're not yet fully conscious of its presence in your subconscious mind. This is where I encourage you to look at your actions instead.

> ▶ Are you acting on things that align with healthy self-worth? Or are you making excuses to avoid taking that action?
>
> ▶ Are you making choices that align with feeling worthy? Or are you making choices that align with feeling unworthy?
>
> ▶ Are you doing everything you genuinely want to do? Or are you holding yourself back?

Your worth is directly reflected in your actions. If you want to get clear on your level of worthiness, review your actions. Review how you're showing up, what you're doing, and who you're being. And yes, this includes the online space where it's easy to hide or pretend to be something you're not in order to gain the validation you seek.

But your worth is NOT found in your social media numbers: it's not found in your follower count, the number of likes or comments in your last post, the number of views on your YouTube channel, or the number of people your posts have reached.

Worthiness is an inside job. What you need to understand is that if you are hunting for self-worth outside of yourself, you'll be hunting forever. No amount of external validation will ever fulfill your desire to feel worthy.

Remember Chanée? She was battling a love/hate relationship with social media when we first met. She found herself posting often because she felt an immense amount of pressure to do so. She questioned everything she posted and was obsessed with looking at her analytics. She would even take the time to look at the names of the people who unsubscribed from her emails. Chanée uncovered that she would be triggered to go into hiding when she felt like her posts and messaging weren't landing or when she noticed people unfollowing.

I asked, "How will you know when your posts and messaging are landing?"

She answered, "I'll have more likes and engagement."

"How do you know when people unfollow you?" I asked.

She answered, "Because I keep an eye on my following count and can see how many people follow and unfollow each day."

That's when I opened her Instagram account on my phone, pulled up her last post, and asked her, "Is this one of the posts that you felt triggered by?"

She said, "Yes."

"What about the thirty-six people who did like this post? Or the three people who commented? Don't they matter?"

And that's when Chanée went quiet. I let her sit with that thought in silence for a while. When she spoke, she said, "It just doesn't feel like enough . . ."

"Enough for who?" I asked.

"Enough for me," she said.

It didn't feel like enough because SHE didn't feel like enough. She depended on her followers to make her feel worthy.

"How many likes or follows will it take for you to feel worthy?" I asked.

"I don't know," she said.

That's when she realized that this was a goal that she'd never reach because she couldn't put a number to it. Her hunt to feel worthy was a hunt with no end in sight. Chanée realized she was posting to validate her worth, and that was the real reason why she had cultivated a love/hate relationship with social media. She wasn't sharing from her heart—she was sharing to appease her audience. She was sharing to satisfy the perception of who she thought her audience needed her to be. And through it all, she lost sight of who she was, what she stood for, and what she was truly here to do.

Your worth is not found in your social media numbers—it's found within you. This is an inside job—an inner-game that you get to play. When you create that sense of worthiness from within, you will gain the confidence to show up as the real you, have the courage to speak your truth, and rise up as the Potent Leader you're here to be.

CHAPTER 22:
WHO YOU BE

There is more power in being versus doing. And yet we've been taught otherwise.

We've been taught to keep ourselves busy, and that "busyness" somehow translates to productivity. But in reality, busyness and productivity are two very different things.

We've been trained to "do" in order to achieve. Do the work, get the degree. Do the work, get the raise. Do the work, get the promotion. Do the work, build the business. But all this "doing" is simply a way to distract yourself from the real work—the inner-work—the work of "being." Because who you're being matters more than what you're doing.

As a society, we've been trained to do, but when were we ever encouraged to BE? When were we shown the power of embodiment? When were we taught how to embrace our beingness?

I started working at the age of fifteen. That was the legal age to work in BC, Canada, and I made sure I jumped on the opportunity to get myself a job right after my birthday. I learned how to juggle school and work among family, friends, and hobbies, and soon I cultivated a habit of taking on as much as possible simply because it was possible.

This is what I knew—it's what I witnessed growing up. My dad created incredible success for himself and was a well-recognized realtor who had accumulated multiple awards and built a solid reputation in the real estate industry. He was constantly "doing": always busy, always in and out of the house, always putting in long hours, always highly committed to his work (while often sacrificing time with us). My dad would sometimes miss my figure skating and rhythmic gymnastics practices, and he would often head right back to work right after dinner, but my mom would always be there. And yet my mom demonstrated constant "busyness" in a different way.

My mom was always running around: taking care of us and overextending herself while doing anything and everything to occupy her time. And when she had nothing to do, she would create something to do, just so she could busy herself.

It's not that I didn't have a great childhood—I did. My parents gave us everything we wanted and took us on trips around the world, which is why my dad worked as hard as he did. But the connection between all of us was missing, and looking back, I can now say that my parents didn't place much thought into who they were being. They were far too distracted with all that they were doing. They were sacrificing their potency.

I grew up in a household that valued *doing* and not *being*. In fact, most Gen Xers and millennials grew up this way. And if you come from an immigrant family like me, you've definitely grown up to value "doing" because we were taught to work HARD for everything we want. But we were never taught (nor were we encouraged) to focus on who we're being, because the emphasis was always on the external world.

By the time I was twenty-one years old, I worked two jobs and owned my own business. At that point, I was an expert at juggling multiple things at once and felt more at ease when I kept myself busy because the busyness distracted me from what was really going on in my life.

I had just entered my first marriage.

My relationship with my middle brother was in shambles.

My parents blamed me for my brother's falling out.

I felt abandoned by my entire extended family due to the situation with my brother and was treated like the black sheep.

My depression and anxiety were escalating.

And my marriage to my first husband wasn't turning out as expected.

Keeping myself busy was simply a way for me to avoid dealing with my feelings. I experienced comfort in the "doing" because it provided me with a sense of relief. Plus, it seemed like the more I did, the more I achieved. But external achievements don't mean shit if you feel like shit, and I felt like shit.

My habit of "doing" continued to get worse as I divorced my first husband, juggled multiple jobs, entered my thirties and started another business. At the age of thirty-three, I had recently married Kevin and moved from Vancouver to LA. I was burnt out, had adrenal fatigue, suffered from insomnia, and had just entered sobriety. Due to the adrenal fatigue, I had to take time off work. And due to the absence of drugs and alcohol, I was faced with my emotions for what felt like the first time ever. I felt like I was forced to just BE with it all.

Some days Kevin would come home and find me starfished on the floor crying, because I had stripped away all my coping mechanisms and didn't know what else to do. Over the following year, I learned how to feel my emotions deeply, without trying to distract myself or numb myself. I learned how to BE with my emotions, and that within itself was a massive game-changer for me.

Through the process of being with my emotions, I learned just how impermanent my feelings were. I learned how to feel what I was feeling without rushing to "make it better" or "make it go away." I learned how to navigate through my emotions, to heal my traumas, and to be present with it all. This process of *being* supported me in understanding the limitless nature of my strength and resilience, which supported me in uncovering my potency.

I swapped out my habit of *doing* for a habit of *being*. I became curious about who I was being and realized that the more I focused on being, the more present I became, and the more present I became, the more I started to embody everything that I was learning. The next few years became a journey of me exploring my being while continuing to build my business.

How deeply would I be willing to let myself feel?

How often was I embodying the words I was sharing?

How much of myself would I be willing to express?

These questions were just some of the things that I was exploring—the things we aren't taught but must learn in order to become our potent selves. And these questions you also get to explore. For the first time in my life, I was being the fullest expression of my message and purpose. Who I was being was congruent with what I was teaching. I was the embodiment of my work, and I was standing in full conviction of who I was and what I offered.

Through this practice of being, my leadership began to shift in the most incredible ways.

Courage was no longer something I tapped into—it was something I embodied.

Confidence was no longer something I chased—it was something I embodied.

Congruence was no longer something I ignored—it was something I embodied.

Conviction was no longer something I lacked—it was something I embodied.

By 2019, I had unleashed my potency by focusing on who I was being. Everything changes when you focus on "being" versus "doing." I started attracting aligned AF clients with joy and ease (feeling completely free to be myself) and started making radical shifts in my business to ensure it felt aligned with me, instead of aligning myself with my business.

This is the magic that comes with the inner-work. When you start to put more focus into who you're being versus what you're doing, you'll unleash your potency. This is a journey of mastering self—a journey with no end, yet it offers infinite expansion and depth as you continue to explore your beingness. And it can begin by asking yourself two questions:

> ▶ Who am I being right now?
>
> This question shifts your focus off what you're doing and helps you gain awareness of who you're being. This awareness provides you with the power to create change.
>
> ▶ Who do I choose to be right now?
>
> This question offers you the opportunity to decide who you want to be, and from there, you get to be that immediately by shifting your actions.

This is a practice, and the more you drop into this practice, the more you'll unleash your potency.

Refuse to get caught up in keeping yourself "busy." Because at the end of the day, it's not about what you're doing—it's about WHO you're being.

PART 3:

POTENCY

CHAPTER 23:
WHAT IS POTENCY?

I spent much of my life trying to fit in. When I was growing up, grade six was when the kids in school started labeling each other as "cool" or "uncool." Sporting black spandex with oversized T-shirts and Keds on my feet every day, hair so long I could sit on it, and a unibrow that would put Frida Kahlo to shame, I was quickly labeled "uncool." From having lots of friends to eating lunch on the stoop by myself, it was a quick and unexpected transition, and one that challenged my sense of worthiness. I realized that if I wanted to fit in, I needed to be more like them—the cool kids.

At age of eleven, I started cultivating my habit of doing everything and anything to fit in and be liked, accepted, and loved by those around me. I asked my mom to take me shopping to buy cooler looking clothes from better name brands. I started talking like the cool kids and became very agreeable with everything they said. And yes . . . I eventually tweezed my unibrow to give myself two actual eyebrows.

High school was no different. I did anything I could to fit in—to be liked, accepted, and loved. Throughout high school was also when I started to rebel against my parents' wishes, including skipping classes, forging my parents' signatures on permission slips, experimenting with dating the wrong types of men, smoking a lot of weed, and drinking beer, coolers, and "killer Kool-Aid." My rebellious nature was an attempt to feel free. At that time in my life, I genuinely believed that I didn't feel free because of my parents. But looking back, I realize that the reason I didn't feel free was because I wasn't giving myself the freedom to be me.

I was repressing the potency that I was born with—the potency that was mine to own—in exchange for fitting in. And my homelife was no different. Even though I was rebelling against my parents, I was also desperate for their love and acceptance. I found myself pretending a lot, wearing different masks for different situations. All to gain the love I craved. All the while diluting my potency.

Fast-forward to May 2014 when I first started my coaching business and had a deeply ingrained habit of doing everything and anything to fit in. I built my business upon the rules of others, doing things their way because, quite frankly, at this point in my life, I didn't even know I had an option to find my own way. I did things to please others as an attempt to gain their love and acceptance. From bending over backward for clients to mimicking other leaders on social media . . . I was completely detached from my potency, and the impact of this detachment on my business was massive.

I found myself pushing a lot and trying to force things to happen . . . until I hit a wall. I lost sight of how I wanted to feel as a leader and, instead, I mimicked other leaders because they had the type of external success that I desired. I wrote my social media posts like them. I experimented with copying their stage presence. I hung out in the same social circles. I went after their goals (because I thought I wanted the same). I kept diluting my potency.

I lost myself in my attempt to be like them, and it did not feel good. I didn't feel good enough to be me because the story in my head told me I wouldn't be loved or accepted as me.

My potency was so watered down that I struggled to attract aligned clients or an aligned audience. Now don't get me wrong . . . I had clients. I had an audience. I even had a Facebook group that organically grew to four thousand people in just over a year. But I was showing up as a completely filtered and edited version of myself and was building a business that didn't feel fully aligned.

That's the thing about potency; it creates alignment. And when your potency is diluted, you'll find yourself attracting misaligned clients (which can leave you feeling unfulfilled with your work), misaligned friendships and relationships (which can leave you feeling disconnected), a misaligned audience (which can leave you feeling as if you need to fight to gain their attention), and misaligned opportunities (which can leave you feeling as if nothing good ever comes your way).

Not feeling free to be you is the same as not giving yourself permission to be free.

Read that again.

I felt shackled to my business, and I was drowning fast. By 2018, I was completely burnt out, my health was deteriorating, and I was ready to quit. The irony of it all was that in 2018, I released my first digital program, entitled "Unleashed & Unapologetic: How to Become a Thought Leader and Create a Cult Following." Yet I myself did not feel completely unleashed and was still apologetic in a lot of ways about who I was. I actually hated the term "cult following" and didn't fully align with all of the content in the program, but I went along with that term and that content because that's what was recommended by my coaches at the time.

I was not embracing my potency nor was I being my potent self. I was living my life for others, denying myself the freedom of my fullest expression, and making myself sick because of it. At the end of 2018, I embarked on my healing journey with plant medicine with the intention to heal my physical, emotional, and mental health. What I didn't realize was that this medicine was exactly what I needed to uncover and unleash my own medicine—a.k.a. my potency. It wasn't until I ventured to that small, remote village of Pahoyan in the Amazon jungle that I truly uncovered my potency.

▼　▼　▼

FROM SELF-CONSCIOUS LEADERSHIP TO POTENT LEADERSHIP

I never used the term *potency* until I felt it within me. It was a feeling that expanded within me as I dropped deeper into the inner-work and shifted from a state of *doing* to *being*. At first, I didn't even recognize that it was there. It seemed to creep up on me until one day, the feeling was so visceral that it could not be ignored. It was an energy that pulsated from deep within my solar plexus chakra and felt like fire—a familiar fire that I hadn't yet experienced in this lifetime. I felt free. For the first time in my life, I felt free. And that freedom tasted like ecstasy.

Everything that I longed for in my entire life was right there, within me, pulsating through me. I felt free to be me, free to speak my truth, free to show up in the fullest expression of my being. FINALLY! I felt free because I had uncovered my potency. And this potency was already creating a positive influence in my life, my business, and my movement. There was more flow, I was attracting aligned clients easily, and I was being a conscious (and not self-conscious) leader. The shift was so gradual that I hadn't noticed the difference in my life until I looked back. I had finally unleashed my medicine onto the world, and it felt incredible.

Potency is the medicine you have to offer when you are being the fullest expression of who you are. It's who you are beneath the masks, the facades, the protective gear, the outdated beliefs, the false fears, the projections, and the expectations. It's the medicine you were born with, yet you diluted over the years due to everything you experienced on your journey. I like to describe the process of unleashing your potency like the process of making ayahuasca.

What you may not know about this ancient, South American, entheogenic medicine is that it is traditionally made from the aya-huasca vine (*Banisteriopsis caapi*), which contains the active MAOIs, and chacruna leaves (*Psychotria viridis*), which contain DMT. These plants are also two totally different species.

The aya vine is pounded to soften it up by removing the outer bark, which breaks the vine into thinner sections, allowing for more extraction of their medicine. Most of the softened vine is then placed in a large cooking pot, which sits on top of a fire. The chacruna leaves are torn into small pieces and added on top, often with another layer of vines, followed by another layer of leaves to fill the pot. That's when the water is added (sometimes as much as forty liters of water). This blend is then cooked over the fire for several hours. Over time, the liquid in the pot begins to reduce, extracting the medicine from each plant into the pot. Once the water has reduced, they add more water to the pot and repeat the reduction process, extracting stronger medi-cine each time. This process is repeated for hours, with prayers, until the liquid is reduced and the medicine is potent.

To unleash your potency, you must pound down the outer masks, facades, protective gear, outdated beliefs, false fears, projections, and expectations to soften you. You then have to tear up the vision that you had once created for yourself to create space for something more aligned. The reduction process is what takes place when you're diving inward, letting the parts of you that aren't true to evaporate, leaving only the essence of who you are—your medicine—your potency.

This process takes time. Just like in the process to create ayahuasca, there are no shortcuts. But once you reduce the medicine within you from a state of diluted potency to potent, you can live your life as you.

No more masks.

No more people-pleasing.

No more chasing false dreams.

And no more trying to be like them.

Your potency allows you to show up as the fullest expression of who you be, helping you make the shift from self-conscious leadership to Potent Leadership.

CHAPTER 24:
BREAKING FREE

"I think the reward for conformity is that everyone likes you except yourself."

—Rita Mae Brown[10]

A nd yet we still do this—we conform, we people-please, we do everything and anything to fit in, including repressing our voice, shoving aside our desires, and losing sight of who we are. For what? To fulfill our basic human need for love and belonging—to gain the love and acceptance of others because we have yet to find that love and acceptance within ourselves. We do this because we want to feel good enough—we want to feel worthy. But your conformity is costing you your potency. It's costing you your gifts, your voice, and your expression.

How long are you willing to continue to sacrifice what's rightfully yours?

Your potency is yours to own—it's yours to ignite, embody, and unleash. This is your medicine that you get to offer yourself and the world. You have a divine right and responsibility to be your potent

---

10. Rita Mae Brown, *Bingo* (New York: Bantam Books, 2008), 259. First published in 1988.

self and to lead with your potent truth. And now, more than ever, the world needs your medicine.

My client Chanée wasn't aware of her potency when we started working together. She was burnt out, lacked clarity, held a scarcity mindset, was incredibly insecure, felt like an imposter, and was suffering deeply from her habit of people-pleasing. She worked with twenty plus one-on-one clients who were paying her next to nothing and, often, she would even "forget" to invoice them, letting payments slide for months on end.

Chanée wasn't aware of her potency. It was almost as if she was afraid of it . . . afraid of what would happen if she dared to show up as her true self. But I saw her potency immediately. I saw her strength, her resiliency, her big heart, her deep passion to serve, and her devotion to the inner-work.

Chanée and I worked together for two years, and throughout those years, I guided her through a deep journey of igniting her potency that began with her coming face-to-face with her trauma, her wounds, and all the pain that she had repressed within her. She had to break down, let shit go, and shatter false beliefs in order to uncover the truth of who she is.

From creating content in order to gain validation from her audience to sharing content that embodies her truth . . .

From pleasing her clients to serving them powerfully . . .

From questioning her every move to listening to the guidance of her intuition . . .

From having a vague and vanilla message to being clear AF about her purpose and who she's here to serve . . .

From working insane hours to working less than twenty hours per week . . .

From doing everything on her own to hiring a team to support her . . .

From being burnt-out to feeling empowered, free, and aligned . . .

Chanée ignited her potency, and it completely shifted the way she was running her business and leading her purpose, because she transformed who she was being.

In 2020, Chanée decided to launch her first mastermind. This was something she had wanted to do for a couple of years, but she always held back because she didn't feel qualified enough to host one. She launched the mastermind with clarity and conviction, embodied her potency, and attracted the most aligned clients she had ever worked with. And she did so with ease and very little strategy. Never had she ever experienced such ease with a launch, nor had she ever launched anything with such clarity and conviction. But this is the power of potency. Chanée was being herself, and by being herself, she gained the attention of those who are truly meant to work with her.

In all the time that I've known Chanée, I've never seen her happier, lighter, or more free. She trusts herself fully, listens to her intuition, and honors her needs. Chanée has become an exceptional leader, one that leads with grace and integrity, and her work is truly impacting the lives of those around her. By igniting her potency, Chanée has unlocked her freedom, reclaimed her voice, and dropped into her potential. Her business has evolved completely, she's living in alignment with her soul purpose, and all other facets of her life have improved—including her marriage.

Igniting your potency is a conscious shift that you get to make. It's a shift that will move you from feeling disempowered to empowered—from living a false identity to living your potency. And this shift can start now.

You've felt the nudge, and just like Chanée, you realize that you've been leading your life and purpose for others. Your soul is beginning to wake up. You're ready to lead your life and purpose for yourself. You recognize that you've been living a false identity. Now, it's time to take ownership of all the ways in which you continue to feed that false identity.

Breaking free is so much more than just taking action—it requires an internal shift. Your programming, mindset, and emotional state have to match the frequency of the actions that you're taking. To truly break free from your cage, you need to understand that you are free—you need to feel free from within, and not rely on your actions to set yourself free.

This is about BEING versus DOING.

Most people operate by doing. In fact, as I've said, our entire society has been trained to DO, and it sounds something like this:

"When I do [ACTION], I'll be [FEELING]."

People think taking the action is enough to change how they feel, but it doesn't happen. Instead, you can be left feeling more caged than ever if you take the action without making the internal shift first.

Freedom is not something you attain by doing something—it's something you become. You must cultivate that sense of freedom from within, and you can do so by following these four steps: awareness, acceptance, ownership, shift.

AWARENESS

First, you need to expand your awareness. You cannot change what you're unwilling to see. If you want freedom, you must be aware of your lack of freedom. You must be aware of all the ways in which you continue to feed your false identity.

ACCEPTANCE

Next, you need to drop into a deep state of acceptance. You cannot change what you're unwilling to accept. You need to accept that you are living a false identity. Keep in mind that acceptance can be tricky because you can be aware of something and still not accept that it is true.

For example, Katie, a client of mine, had been struggling with bulimia for over a decade. She was incredibly unhappy with her body image and became obsessed with being fit. No matter what she did, she couldn't achieve her version of looking fit. She had shared with me that all she wanted was to feel confident enough to run on the beach in her sports bra and no shirt—this was her vision of freedom. Katie was aware that she did not look the way she wanted to look, but she hadn't accepted where she was at.

In a coaching session, I asked Katie: "Do you accept how you look?"

She looked at me with wide eyes filled with curiosity and fear, and she replied back, "Why would I accept how I look? If I accept how I look, that means that I'd be happy with how I looked and would stop trying to be fit."

Katie couldn't achieve her goal of being fit because she was unwilling to accept how she looked. She continued to lean into destructive behaviors as an attempt to look a certain way while refusing to look at herself in the mirror, living a false identity.

I asked her to stand in front of the mirror for two minutes each morning and look at herself from head to toe with as much compassion and love as possible. She did this for a week straight, and things began to shift. As excruciatingly difficult as it was to do this exercise each morning, she did it, and by doing so, she started to accept her body, and in turn, she accepted herself.

Soon after that, Katie broke free from her decade-long battle with bulimia and started running on the beach in just her sports bra and shorts. She cultivated freedom within herself by accepting where she was at. And today, she is devoted to her health and well-being, is an avid surfer and CrossFitter, loves her body, and has found her purpose supporting others in their health journeys.

Awareness is NOT the same as acceptance. Acceptance comes after awareness. You need to accept where you are prior to getting to where you want to be. And once you do that, you get to take responsibility for where you are (a.k.a. own your shit).

The moment you own your shit is the moment you'll gain the power to break free.

OWNERSHIP

When you refuse to take ownership, you're denying yourself of your growth while keeping yourself stuck in a victim mentality. It's easy to place blame. In fact, it's very comfortable to live in a victim mentality because you don't have to take responsibility for anything. You get comfortable in your misery. You get comfortable blaming others and your circumstances.

What's hard is seeing all the ways in which you are showing up in your false identity because when you do, you'll realize that you are the one who constructed it (which can be a tough pill to swallow). You are responsible for creating the changes you seek as you uncover your truth and unleash your potency.

But change feels so hard, especially when you've become accustomed to living in denial with your unconscious thoughts and actions on autopilot. Change feels hard because it requires a new thought process that you have to consciously create and new actions that you have to consciously take.

As crazy as this sounds, you get comfortable in your discomfort because it's easy to live on autopilot. But if you truly want to achieve freedom, you have to open your eyes and consciously own your shit. The moment you own your shit is the moment you gain the power to create change and become free.

Owning my shit changed everything. I remember the exact moment that I finally opened my eyes wide enough to see past my finger-pointing ways. It was when I hit rock bottom in 2012. My thoughts and actions led me to that rock bottom moment, and if I truly wanted to experience life differently, I had to take ownership. It was literally the moment that I began to experience freedom.

There are things that you have yet to take ownership of in your life. You don't have to wait until rock bottom to see all the ways in which you're playing a false identity—choose to see that now. Because the moment you own your shit is the moment you gain the power to break free.

Once you take ownership for one thing, you'll start to see another thing, and another, and another. You'll start to see every single choice, action, thought, fear, and belief that has helped you construct your false identity. **You can't unsee what you now see.** From here on out, you can continue to live your false identity, knowing that you're diluting your potency, or you can make a conscious shift to break free by shifting your thoughts and your actions to offer you a new outcome.

SHIFT

The shift first takes place in your mind. You need to believe different to act different. You need to get uncomfortable by consciously choosing your beliefs. Your beliefs influence your thoughts, so by choosing your beliefs, you begin to shift your thoughts. This shift in your mind then leads to shifts in your behavior, your habits, your choices, your decisions, and your actions. You have to believe something different in order to think differently, and you have to think differently in order to be different.

4 STEPS TO FREEDOM

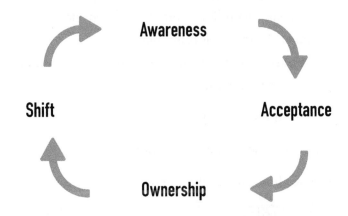

Awareness

Acceptance

Ownership

Shift

Instead of depending on others to deconstruct your false identity for you *(hello, victim mentality)*, start relying on yourself to pick up the sledgehammer and break free.

Now that you've heightened your awareness, accepted where you're at, owned your shit, and created the necessary shifts, you find yourself living your true identity because you feel free from within.

You've freed yourself from your old programming, mindset, and emotional state. You have designed a new way of being—a way that has you embodying your potency and feeling free. But refuse to become complacent in this phase. Our world and our society are not built to leave you feeling free—it's built to keep you from feeling safe enough to be yourself.

We live in a world with expectations, rules, regulations, restrictions—all of which can sway you from feeling free. The outside world may leave you feeling as if you need to shrink yourself to fit in, or quiet your voice, or conform to others, or obey the conventional rules, or be a certain way in order to be accepted. But when you focus on embodying freedom, you will create that acceptance within and will never find yourself living a false identity again.

To this day, Chanée is living her life as her most potent self, experiencing freedom from within, and living her purpose on her own terms. She is being the fullest expression of who she is and as such, she's designing a life that feels fully aligned.

Freedom is truly a way of being—it's a choice that you consciously make each and every single day.

You get to choose to use your voice.

You get to choose to show up in your potency.

You get to choose to be who you be.

That's true freedom.

CHAPTER 25:
THE STORIES YOU TELL YOURSELF

J ess and I first connected on Instagram in the summer of 2019. She had shared one of my posts, and we dove into a conversation in our messages. A day after that, Jess applied to attend my Activation Retreat, which marked the beginning of our incredible journey together.

Just one month prior, Jess had left her corporate job to pursue her purpose full-time. She was at a pivotal moment in her life when we connected at that retreat, one that would have her coming face-to-face with the stories she had continued to tell herself.

From our very first session, prior to the retreat, I learned that the Jess presented to the world was very different from who she actually is. In that initial one-hour session, Jess shared her undeniable passion for supporting service providers in building six-figure businesses, as this had been her own journey. She also shared that she wanted to start incorporating mindset work and personal development into her programs because she knew that offering her clients strategy alone wasn't enough to support them . . . but she had yet to implement this. When I asked her why she hadn't yet incorporated mindset and personal development into her programs, she answered, "I don't want them to think I'm crazy."

"Who are you referring to when you say 'them'?" I asked.

"My family and my close friends. I don't want them to think I've gone off the deep end."

Jess then went on to share about her religious upbringing, and how she was taught to show up a certain way, be a certain way, and speak a certain way in order to be loved and accepted by her family and her religion. Jess also shared with me that since she was a child, she had been told things like "you're too loud," "you're too abrasive," "you're not being proper," and "this is not how a lady acts." Her current spiritual beliefs didn't align with her religious upbringing, and she found herself diluting her potency just so she could feel loved and accepted.

That's when Jess went on to say, "I fear being too much for my husband. I fear being too loud, too outspoken, too independent, or too 'woo-woo' for him."

It was apparent to me then that Jess is an incredibly talented business strategist with a substantial amount of experience. She's also a very gifted mindset and personal development coach who deeply cares about helping her clients. But she was holding herself back due to the stories from her past—the stories that she continued to tell herself. She was holding herself back because she believed that she was "too much" for the people she loved. This wasn't only happening in her business, but in her personal life too.

And maybe you can relate. . .

We become the expression of the stories we tell ourselves.

These stories create barriers that prevent us from seeing our truth—our potency. Jess had written a story based on her traumas, not her potential, and there's a big difference between the two.

When you base your story on your trauma, you're writing from a place of victimization—as if the world will always work against you. You hold onto the pain and expect more to come, dismissing the parts of your story that speak to your potential and your ability to work through your shit. When you write your story from your trauma, you become blind to your potency.

But when you base your story on your potential, you're writing from a place of empowerment, knowing you have control over your life. You honor your trauma, recognize your growth, celebrate your successes, and see the possibilities. You become aware of your potency.

Jess's life was in shambles when we first connected. Not only was she holding herself back in her business, but also her marriage was on the rocks, and she was experiencing depression and anxiety daily. She was diluting her potency as a way to feel loved and accepted by her family and her husband, and she felt like she was constantly living life as an imposter, with the dial turned way down. Jess's deepest fear wasn't the fear of being "too much"; it was the fear of being abandoned for being too much. Due to this, she had cultivated a habit of running away from her trauma. It was a self-preservation mechanism that kept her feeling safe, but it also provided her with a false sense of freedom because being alone felt like the only time she could really be herself. Jess had booked a solo trip to Bali right after the Activation Retreat because her life at home felt overwhelming. But what took place at the retreat changed everything.

During those four days in our retreat home, tucked away in the forest, Jess came face-to-face with her trauma, and I wasn't letting her run away. In fact, I had her face her trauma head-on. On the second day of the retreat, after leading them through a powerful evening ceremony of breath work (a tool that I use to support clients in working through their traumas while grounding into their bodies), we all sat in a circle on the floor for integration (an opportunity for everyone to share about their experience from the ceremony night before).

The first few people shared, referring to their experiences as "beautiful" and "powerful." When it came time for Jess to share, I could sense that she was in a different state.

"I'm fucking pissed," she said. I remained quiet, maintaining eye contact while offering her the space to expand on what she just said.

"I'm fucking pissed that everyone had this life-changing experience during our breath work ceremony, and I struggled the entire time. I felt like I couldn't let go and surrender to the experience," she said.

It was true. Jess had struggled that night during our breath work ceremony. She was experiencing tetany, which is when parts of the body feel stiff or cramped. This can happen during breath work due to the alkalization process that occurs during a period of prolonged, deep breathing. Aside from the science behind tetany and breath work, there's also a deeper reason for this to occur.

Perhaps you've heard the saying "We hold our issues in our tissues." But what you may not know is the truth behind this saying. Our traumas, stories, habits, and beliefs are held within our bodies. This is why you can go twenty years without riding a bike only to pick up a bike and ride it again. It's called muscle memory. Which means that the inner-work isn't just about mindset, it's also about working through your trauma through your body, and breath work is a way to make that happen.

Throughout the breath work ceremony, I had been guiding Jess to let go—to surrender to the process and be with all that she was feeling. But she continued to resist, which only worsened the tetany in her body. That next morning during integration, she told us that she was angry from the experience, but the truth was . . . she was angry at herself.

After hearing her share about how pissed off she was, I stood up and asked her to come with me. Together, we walked to the other side of the room, where I placed her in front of a mirror and asked her to look herself in the eyes and express her anger toward herself. At first, she was scared. But she went into the exercise headfirst and started expressing her anger.

"I'm angry at myself for not doing it right. I'm angry at myself for not letting go. I'm angry at myself for not being able to surrender to the experience. I'm angry at myself for holding myself back . . ."

She continued to express her anger, escalating her voice each time until she was yelling at her reflection in the mirror.

"I'm angry at myself for feeling as if I'm too much." And that's when she softened, and her anger turned to sadness.

We continued through this process of uncovering the stories that she held onto, working through anger, sadness, and grief—allowing her the space to fully express herself without holding anything back. And by the end of that exercise, you could feel the weight being lifted off her shoulders.

The stories you tell yourself can serve you or work against you. And in this case with Jess, her stories were working against her. Up until that moment, she had been living her life with a diluted potency due to her fear of being abandoned by her family and her husband. She was pretending to be who she thought they wanted her to be, showing up with the dial turned way down. And the truth was . . . due to her upbringing, she just assumed that her husband wouldn't accept her in her potency, which was why she found herself in a marriage that was in shambles.

Jess and I ended up working together for a year, and through-out that time we tackled her stories head-on, shifted her beliefs, and worked through the trauma she associated with being "too much." Along with the inner-work, I also supported her in redesigning her business to match her potency so she could experience the freedom of being who she is in all that she was doing.

Remember that solo trip I told you about? Jess did end up going on that solo trip, but also used that as an opportunity to work on herself while working up the courage to start expressing herself fully in her life and with her husband.

After our one-year experience together, Jess found herself in a place within her marriage where she felt fully expressed, fully seen, and fully loved for all that she is. She was no longer battling depression and anxiety, she was showing up for her business and clients with the dial turned way up, her marketing became an expression of who she is, and she was experiencing more freedom than ever before.

Today, Jess is one of the most Potent Leaders I know. She stands with conviction in her purpose, owns her voice and presence, and is fully expressed in every way possible. Her business continues to reflect her truth, her audience and visibility has grown exponentially, and she has fully merged mindset, personal development, and "woo" into her programs. In addition to that, Jess is the happiest she's ever been because she's living as the fullest expression of who she is. No more holding back or turning the dial down. Jess owns her potency and is living her truth.

Jess, like many of my clients, was holding herself back from show-ing the world (and herself) who she be. But when she uncovered the stories that were driving her actions and behavior, she shifted from being led by her trauma to being led by her potential.

Jess shifted her story, and in doing so, she unlocked her potential and embodied her potency.

Be aware of the stories that you tell yourself, because these are the stories that will influence you to dilute your potency or embody your potency.

> ▶ What stories are you telling yourself?
> ▶ And are these stories influencing you to dilute your potency or embody your potency?

CHAPTER 26:
DARE TO BE SEEN

"What will people think?!"

These words pierced through the phone, threatening to shatter my confidence.

It was 2014, and I was on the phone with my dad, who had just called to let me know that he didn't approve of me sharing my story online with such transparency.

I had just started sharing my story publicly and was learning how to lean into my voice, uncovering my potency for what felt like the first time . . . and it was heartbreaking to hear that my dad didn't approve—the man whose approval I had been chasing my entire life.

I held the phone with shaky hands, heart racing, anxiety rising, and feeling the eleven-year-old version of myself creep in.

"What WILL people think?" These words rippled inside my head.

I am a Punjabi, Sikh woman . . . coming from a very conservative culture . . . talking about my addiction . . . talking about my suicide attempt . . . talking about my abusive relationships . . . talking about my depression and anxiety . . . PUBLICLY.

I felt scared, upset, angry, frustrated, and sad that I didn't have my dad's approval. Hands still shaking, I gripped the phone tightly and heard my dad say,

"You don't need to share your story to help people."

That's when something clicked. The fire within me ignited and I remembered WHY I was doing this and what initiated me into this work.

"Yes, I do. Dad, I have to share my story so people understand they're not alone . . . like I felt when I was going through this. I don't need you to understand or accept why I'm doing this."

And that was that. I ended the conversation with him still disapproving of my actions, and I chose to make peace with that because I understood why I was speaking up. I was in a state of full acceptance with myself.

I continued to share my story on stages and podcasts.

I continued to create raw YouTube videos.

I continued to be transparent on social media.

I continued to show up, be visible, and create a movement with my message, all while letting myself be seen.

And today, I stand before you as a happy, successful, six-figure Potent Leadership Guide with a dad who expresses how proud he is of me almost every single week.

Choosing to be seen is THE reason I was able to create my success quickly. In a world where everyone is fighting to be seen, heard, and understood . . . showing up from a place of raw authenticity makes ALL the difference because it offers an opportunity for your audience to see themselves in you, which creates a feeling of connection. But when you're only striving for visibility, you'll swap out vulnerability and transparency for performing and pretending because you'll do anything to get the spotlight on you.

I could have let my fear of judgment hold me back . . .

I could have listened to my dad . . .

I could have hidden and stayed quiet . . .

But I knew that my story has the power to impact others, and I am here to SERVE and give the world a voice.

My purpose is greater than my fear.

We ALL experience the fear of judgment—after all, we're human, and we share the basic human need for love and belonging. When you put yourself out there, you open yourself up to being judged and disliked. But you also open yourself up to creating connection and impact—to supporting your audience, community, and clients in incredibly powerful ways.

Isn't that worth the judgments?

In the words of my friend and publicity expert, Selena Soo: *"If you want to help people, they need to know you exist."*[11]

The people you're here to serve need to know you—the real you. Refuse to let your fears hold you back from changing the world.

Rise up.

Speak up.

Be visible.

And dare to be seen.

---

11. Selena Soo, publicity expert (n.d.), https://www.selenasoo.com.

Give the people you're here to serve a real opportunity to see you and connect with the real you. But remember, being visible is not the same thing as being seen.

Consider this. . .

> ▶ Is your desire to gain visibility actually just be a desire to feel significant?
>
> ▶ Are you seeking more followers because you think that this will help you establish yourself as an expert?
>
> ▶ Are you seeking more attention to your work because you think that this will help validate what you're doing?
>
> ▶ Are you seeking more eyes on your movement because you think that this will help you gain the success you desire?

You want the spotlight on you because this will help you feel significant, but in reality, this will create a false sense of significance. The significance that you're seeking will not come through what marketers refer to as "visibility." You need to cultivate that sense of significance within yourself.

Let's start with the difference between external and internal significance . . .

External significance is when you want to be SEEN as a leader.

Internal significance is when you are BEING a leader.

External significance is when you're chasing validation, approval, and acknowledgment. Whereas internal significance is when you're creating that validation, approval, and acknowledgment within yourself.

You can achieve visibility and still not feel seen. To be honest, it's pretty damn easy to achieve visibility. All you must do is follow one of many cookie-cutter strategies to put yourself out there, get featured online (which you can easily pay for), get booked on podcasts, speak on stages (which includes "pay to play"), and voila, you've achieved visibility! But these strategies often don't account for your uniqueness—they don't support authenticity and transparency. Instead, these strategies ask you to show up in a certain way to be perceived in a certain way to achieve a certain result, causing you to dilute your potency.

These strategies definitely work and will provide you with the "wins" you need to share "as featured in" logos on your website home page and Instagram bio. But how authentic is it to share "as featured in ABC News" when you were interviewed to talk about something that has absolutely nothing to do with your business, mission, or movement?

You're chasing significance through visibility when what you're really seeking is to feel seen.

You want to feel seen for the good work that you're doing.

You want to feel seen for all the effort and energy that you've put into yourself and what you're building.

You want to feel seen as the leader you know you are.

You want to feel seen, period. And that won't happen through a cookie-cutter strategy that is focused on helping you manufacture a sense of significance and validation. The only way you'll feel seen is by doing the inner-work to see yourself and establish inner-significance.

This is the way of the Potent Leader.

CHAPTER 27:
SOCIAL MEDIA FOR SOCIAL GOOD

Today, 45 percent of the world's population is on social media. And with the world's population sitting at just over 7.7 billion,[12] that's 3.5 billion people using social media. Since the inception of social media in 1997, there's been astronomical growth in users. What we're seeing online is a real global community. With the rise of social media, what we're also experiencing as a collective is a rise in empathy and compassion and a deepened desire for connection.

We're experiencing a rise in empathy and compassion because we can now see what's taking place on the other side of the world. War, famine, poverty, the fires in the Amazon jungle, animals threatened to become extinct, the Great Pacific Garbage Patch . . . we have front row seats to view what is happening to our planet and our collective, and this is influencing us to take more action than ever to serve, support, and strengthen our world.

---

12. "World Population Prospects 2019 Highlights, (2019 revision)," United Nations, Department of Economic and Social Affairs, Population division, https://population.un.org/wpp/Publications /Files/WPP2019_Highlights.pdf.

We're experiencing a deepened desire for connection because as connected as we all are, we're actually feeling more disconnected than ever. We have access to the world in our pockets and we have the power to connect with each other just by the taps of our thumbs, and yet, we're connecting less with each other in person. Social media has become a distraction that can often seem more interesting than real life. But it doesn't have to be this way.

What if we used social media for social good?

What if we used social media to better ourselves, our planet, and our collective?

What if we used social media with the intention to serve, support, and strengthen our world?

What if we used social media to connect—*really connect*—with each other?

Imagine what would become possible . . . and imagine how much better your relationship with social media would feel.

With 45 percent of the world's population on social media, you have the power to better our world, and that starts with you bettering yourself. This is about being authentic versus fake AF . . . being vulnerable versus guarded . . . being transparent versus manipulative.

This is about using social media as a Potent Leader.

What drives you to use social media? Let's be real, you don't have to be on social media, but you choose to be because you see this as a way for you to share your message and gain more eyes on your movement.

But there are much deeper motives at play—in fact, there are seven motives for social media: Stability, Acceptance, Significance, Esteem, Evolution, Purpose, Humanity.

MOTIVE #1: STABILITY

You're using social media to create a sense of security and certainty in your life. There's a perceived level of control with social media, and you're using that to build a foundation for yourself and your purpose. Just think about how much effort you put into coming up with the perfect bios or designing the perfect header images or writing the perfect captions—all for the sole purpose of providing you with a sense of security in who you are and what you're here to do.

"I am safe."

MOTIVE #2: ACCEPTANCE

You're using social media to feel as if you belong to a community and are loved by that community. With 3.5 billion users, your presence on social media presents a sense of belonging because your profile immediately makes you a member of the global community. Even those who feel like outcasts in real life can find a community online. You're leaning into the leadership community to create a sense of validation and belonging.

"I belong."

MOTIVE #3: SIGNIFICANCE

You're using social media to establish status and a sense of importance. You do this through your bio, your captions, your photos, and your videos. And you're using the title of "leader" to be perceived as someone who is significant. In fact, everything you share is somehow contributing to feeling significant because you want to know that your life matters.

"I matter."

MOTIVE #4: ESTEEM

You're using social media to boost self-worth and to feel validated by others. Every positive interaction on social media—whether it be a "like," a "follow", a "comment" or a "share"—gives you a hit of dopamine, which leaves you feeling more worthy and validated by your audience. And the external recognition that you gain through your perception as a leader fuels your self-esteem.

"I am worthy."

MOTIVE #5: EVOLUTION

You're using social media and leaning into your role as a leader to learn new things, to take charge of your personal growth, and to create momentum in your evolution. You're watching videos by those you admire, reading posts by those who inspire you, and are taking your evolution into your own hands by capitalizing on the abundance of do-it-yourself content and digital information.

"I am growing (not dying)."

MOTIVE #6: PURPOSE

You're using social media to feel as if you're living to your potential. You're sharing your message and your story and using the platform as a way to fulfill your purpose so you can, in turn, feel fulfilled.

"I am fulfilled."

MOTIVE #7: HUMANITY

You're using your role as a leader to serve others and do good in the world. You have a deep desire to influence change because you believe that you can. You want to help move the conscious collective forward and are using your social media networks to promote humanity with the type of content you choose to produce and share.

"I am of service."

> ▶ So, what's really driving you? Which of these seven motives best describes how you show up on social media?

Potent Leadership isn't about "doing," nor is it about what you've achieved, what you have, or who you surround yourself with. Potent Leadership is about you, being the fullest expression of who you be, showing up unapologetically as the leader that you are, standing in full conviction of your worth, your gifts, and your purpose (offline AND online). When you own your potency, you give yourself the freedom to be you. And in a digital world that makes it so tempting to be like everyone else, your potency is the medicine that humanity needs to break their feeds and interrupt their habit of scrolling.

Today's technology offers you the opportunity to reach people around the globe. Are you using that opportunity to create meaningful connections? Or are you using it to collect "followers"?

Social media networks had the old paradigm of leadership in mind when they adopted the word *followers*. Similarly, your email list, text messaging service, and YouTube channel follow the old paradigm by using the word *subscribers*. As we redefine leadership and enter a new paradigm, it's important to note that what is becoming more widely welcomed as a term is "leaders creating leaders" mentality versus an "I lead, you follow" mentality. I invite you to take this one step further and adopt a "leaders leading leaders" mentality. As such, it's time for you to reframe the way in which you view and refer to your followers.

Old paradigm for leadership = Followers
New paradigm for leadership = Audience
Potent paradigm for leadership = Community

Behind every single number is a human being—a person who made the conscious decision to follow you or subscribe to your content, and that matters. It matters because, as a Potent Leader, you get to help them feel as though they belong to your movement. After all, we're all seeking a place to belong and when someone feels as though they are part of what you are creating, they will become that much more loyal—or as Pat Flynn[13] likes to call them, they'll become a Superfan.

But let's be real . . . the temptation to posture, to self-edit, to pretend, and to please those around you can still come up, even after you've unleashed your potency. Like I mentioned before, digital technology is built to feed your addiction for attention, approval, and likes. I still get tempted, which is why I created a set of eight principles for Potent Leadership—principles that if followed, will support you in remaining grounded in your potency.

---

13. Pat Flynn, *Superfans* (San Diego: Get Smart Books, 2019). See also https://patflynn.com/books.

PRINCIPLE #1:
I SHARE MY TRUTH, EVEN AT THE RISK OF LOSING FOLLOWERS.

We talk about truth a lot; yet, truth is subjective. Your truth may differ from my truth, and that's okay. What's not okay is holding back due to your fear of losing followers. What's not okay is biting your tongue due to your fear of being canceled or shamed. What's not okay is sharing false truths just to please those around you. What's not okay is manipulating your truth in order to maintain an image. What's not okay is diluting your potency.

As a Potent Leader, you're not here to paint a pretty picture—you're here to pave the way, and that requires you to share your truth. If you find this difficult, it comes down to two things: your fear of how people will react (which stems from your need for love and belonging), or your lack of trust in yourself. Get real about your fears, and start trusting your truth. Sharing your truth will support you in attracting an aligned community—people who value what you value and people who appreciate what you have to say. And I know this sounds cliché, but the ones who unfollow you are the ones who aren't meant to be in your community, nor are they the ones you're meant to serve. Remember, potency is an amplification process. No more dilution, and that includes dilution within your community. You get to give yourself the freedom of sharing your truth.

PRINCIPLE #2:
I SPEAK UP WHEN I'M READY TO SPEAK UP, AND NOT WHEN I FEEL PRESSURED TO OR SHAMED INTO SPEAKING UP.

Shame and cancel culture have made it feel even harder to remain grounded in your potency: from people sliding into your DMs (shaming you about not speaking up over a current social justice matter), to the internal pressure that you place on yourself to speak up immediately when you see other leaders doing so. But are you really ready to speak up? Do you understand enough to take a stand? Have you taken the time to sort through the information, use your discernment, and uncover your truth in this matter? If the answer is no, allow yourself the freedom to dive deeper into the issue before speaking up to ensure that you respond versus react.

When #BLM hit the headlines in 2020, many of my clients were feeling it. Some spoke up immediately because it felt right for them to do so and they were grounded in their truth, while others were completely rocked by it, feeling stunned, questioning what was going on, getting bombarded by DMs from their own clients and followers shaming them for not saying anything, feeling the internal pressure to speak up, all while not knowing what to say. One of my clients, Kendra, felt this deeply. As a successful white woman in a position of leadership, she was targeted by many people and received a backlash of DMs shaming her for not saying anything. We spoke about this in a mentorship session, and I realized that it wasn't that she didn't want to speak up about it—she had yet to really research the matter for herself to understand how she truly felt about it. She was still processing the entire event and felt that she didn't yet know enough to contribute her voice. As such, I told her something that I want you to remember. I said: "It's okay to give yourself the space to process this information and educate yourself on what's going on. And, as a leader, it's important for you to acknowledge what happened and address where you're at in this process. Be real. This isn't about getting it 'right.'" And she did. The next day, Kendra shared a post acknowledging the headlines, humbly sharing that she didn't know enough about the events that were taking place, and that she would be doing more research into this.

As a Potent Leader, it's crucial that you show up, AND it's crucial that you are grounded in what you're saying. Rather than trying to get it right, you must share truthfully and authentically. You must be transparent about what you don't know because this isn't about trying to maintain an image—this is about being a Potent Leader. When you find yourself in these situations (not clear on what to say just yet, wanting the space to research the matter for yourself first), give yourself that space, AND speak up by acknowledging what's taken place and being real about where you're at.

PRINCIPLE #3:

I TALK ABOUT WHAT'S IMPORTANT TO ME, EVEN IF THAT MEANS BREAKING FREE FROM MY CONTENT STYLE AND STRATEGY.

Refuse to let your online image dictate how you share. Refuse to get caught up in making your grid perfect or in sticking to your email content style or text messaging strategy. Let your content, messaging, and communication be a reflection of who you be—let it be a reflection of your potency.

I've adopted grid styles and content strategies—hell, I used to create content strategies for brands and companies when I ran my own social media marketing agency. But what I've learned through all of this is that there is no freedom in sticking to a set of rules. The styles that you adopt can definitely elevate your brand image, and the strategies that you put into place can definitely boost your numbers, but all of this can also dilute your potency by holding you hostage to a certain set of parameters. Where's the freedom in that?

Imagine hearing about a major event in our world and not being able to speak on it because today you're scheduled to share your latest podcast episode. Imagine receiving earth-shattering news and not feeling free to talk about it because today you're supposed to announce your latest product launch. Is this really leadership?

You have the freedom to break free from your content style and strategy. You get to make the conscious decision to do so. And as a Potent Leader, it's your responsibility to lead by being, not by an image that you're trying to maintain.

PRINCIPLE #4:
I SEEK TO UNDERSTAND THOSE WITH DIFFERENT BELIEFS, NOT IMPULSIVELY REACT TO THEM.

Since when is leadership about being stubborn in your beliefs? Since when is leadership about not listening to others? Or not practicing compassion? Or not being open-minded? Or not thinking critically? Since when is leadership about reacting to those who hold different beliefs than you?

The online space is the perfect breeding ground for volatility. Typing on a shiny black screen can dehumanize conversations, which leads to reactivity in communication. What you have to remember is that there will always be those who believe differently, think differently, and act differently. There will always be people who believe the polar opposite of what you do.

As a Potent Leader, you can stand firmly in your beliefs while still remaining open to seeing things differently. You can believe one thing while seeking to understand why others believe something different.

Instead of reacting to those with different political views, seek to understand why they view things the way that they do.

Instead of reacting to those with different theories on what's taking place in our world, seek to understand their theories.

By seeking to understand, you're keeping the conversation open instead of shutting it down. You're creating a space for connection. You're giving others the opportunity to feel heard, seen, and acknowledged for their beliefs instead of pushing them away. This is Potent Leadership.

PRINCIPLE #5:
I ACKNOWLEDGE WHAT I DON'T KNOW INSTEAD OF PRETENDING TO BE AN EXPERT WHO KNOWS IT ALL.

FACT: You don't know everything. And if you're still trying to persuade yourself into thinking that you do, I suggest you reread this book from the beginning.

Potent Leadership isn't about knowing all the answers—it's about being humble enough to admit that you don't know everything and courageous enough to address what you don't know.

The saying "Fake it until you make it" is the old paradigm of leadership. Potent Leadership is about embodying it until you are it. Don't pretend to know all the answers. Acknowledge what you don't know. If it's important to you, make the effort to know it. After all, mastery isn't an end goal—it's a journey. You are a student first. When you adopt that mentality, you open yourself to leading with authenticity and integrity.

PRINCIPLE #6:
I OWN MY SHIT PUBLICLY INSTEAD OF DISMISSING MY FAULTS TO MAINTAIN AN IMAGE.

I can't even tell you how many times I've sent out an "oh shit!" email to my community. Whether it was a "Oh shit! Here's the right link" email, or an "Oh shit! I fucked up" email, or an "Oh shit! That wasn't supposed to go out today" email . . . there have been countless emails sent. Many times I've been wrong in a social media post, or I misquoted something online, and then someone corrected me.

Can it be embarrassing to say the wrong thing or share a broken link? For sure, if you let it be. But as a Potent Leader, it's important that you do not let your ego take the lead. What you must realize is that the more you try to maintain an image, the harder it becomes for your community to connect with you because perfection doesn't feel real. There is honor in humility.

You will fuck up. It's inevitable. But brushing your fuckups under the rug lacks integrity. You're better than that. Choose to own your shit publicly. Choose to admit when you're wrong so you can rehumanize your leadership.

PRINCIPLE #7:
I FOCUS ON SHARING, NOT PERSUADING OR CONVINCING.

Stop using your platform to persuade others. Stop trying to convince others of your beliefs. Instead, focus on sharing. As I've mentioned before, there will always be those who think and believe differently. Your duty as a leader isn't to get them on "your side." This is the old paradigm of leadership, the paradigm that has you standing on a pedestal with your megaphone, screaming at your audience in an attempt to get them to listen. That is not your job. Your job is to own your potency and lead.

Focus on sharing.

Share your truth. Share your opinions. Share your beliefs. Share your knowledge. Share your wisdom. And share without the expectation to change their minds or persuade them to think differently or convince them to do things your way.

PRINCIPLE #8:
I CHOOSE TO BE WHO I AM WITH MY AUDIENCE, AND NOT A PERFORMER TRYING TO CONTROL HOW I'M BEING PERCEIVED.

This is vital to your potency. Remember what I said about influencership versus leadership? You're not here to paint a pretty picture—you're here to pave the way. You need to be the fullest expression of everything you teach, preach, and share. This is about you, owning who you be.

Your aligned audience does not want to see another cookie-cutter leader—they want to see you, because they need to see themselves in you. You need to give your audience the opportunity to get to know the real you. You need to give them the opportunity to experience your potency, and that can't happen when you're trying to control how you're being perceived.

I remember performing when I first started out as a coach. I was obsessed with how I was being perceived and putting way too much time and energy into trying to control my image. All this did was help me attract a misaligned audience while leaving me feeling drained, disconnected, and unseen.

After devoting myself to the inner-work and unleashing my potency, I started showing up as me with my audience, which helped me build a real community around my movement. I started sharing all sides of myself and my potency, standing unapologetically as the leader that I am, which made it easy to attract an aligned audience of people I am here to serve—people who were truly interested in being part of my movement—people who wanted to invest in my services and programs. And I was left feeling energized, connected, seen, and above all else, free.

The temptation to posture, to self-edit, to pretend, and to please those around you is real, especially in social media. But that's NOT leadership. You're not here to perform—you're here to lead. And you're here to lead as the fullest expression of who you be. You're here to lead with your potency.

CHAPTER 28:
POTENT LEADERSHIP

Most leaders who claim to be conscious leaders are still leading in self-conscious ways. Let me be straight with you: being "conscious" is not a claim—it's a state of being. And many leaders are simply claiming that they are conscious as an attempt to be perceived that way. They're missing one crucial ingredient to consciousness, and that's potency.

Since you're reading this book, I'm going to assume that you see yourself as a conscious leader. I'm also going to assume that you're tired of all the bullshit pretending, and you're seeking to show up as your authentic, transparent, and potent self.

Let's break it down . . .

To be conscious is to be aware of who you're being, what you're doing, and the world around you.

To be a leader is to act as a guide— to show or lead the way.

What I want you to realize is that you can't be a conscious leader and pretend at the same time. You pretend because you're too self-conscious to show up as you. When you're showing up as a self-conscious leader, you're leading unconsciously, meaning that you're unaware of who you're being, what you're doing, and the world around you. You're caught up in trying to control how you're being perceived, diluting your potency, losing sight of who you are and the impact that you're creating on those around you.

One of my mentors claimed to be a conscious leader. He has an enormous presence online, is a sought-after speaker, and seemed to have everything that I wanted. So, I chose to work with him in an intimate, one-on-one container that consisted of in-person immersives and calls. This was a huge investment for me and one I truly felt excited about.

Now before I go any further, please know that we ALL do this. I was leading my life unconsciously for years. This does not make us good or bad—it simply is part of our journeys. We're programmed to run on autopilot and fuel our basic human needs with any means necessary, including our need for love and belonging. We can be a conscious being with unconscious behaviors. As I share this story, know that I stand here today with deep love, appreciation, and respect for this mentor: for who he is, and for the journey that he is on. After all, we're all mirrors for each other.

My first in-person immersive with this mentor was an amazing experience that I gained a lot out of, and part of what I gained was witnessing a live example of a self-conscious leader claiming to be conscious. We were there with his team who were also there to support me. But while his team would guide me through something, he often interjected when it wasn't at all necessary, and it seemed to come from a place of needing to prove himself—from not fully trusting himself. To be honest, all his interjecting was throwing me off the guidance that I was already receiving from his team.

At one point, when I was deep in strategy creation with his team, I noticed that another team member had pulled out his phone on the other side of the room in front of me. My mentor was seated to my far left, quietly observing, but as soon as the phone came out, he jumped up with his laptop, positioned himself closer to me, and began to interject again, throwing us off-topic while we were in the midst of an insightful discussion. That's when I heard the camera phone go off.

Self-conscious leaders are more concerned with their image than the impact that they're creating. And this mentor was definitely and unconsciously wrapped up in his image, too fixated on creating picture-perfect moments to even notice the impact that this had on me, his client, the person who had chosen to invest her time, energy, love, and resources into this container.

I'm certain that this was not an intentional act by any means. After all, how can we be intentional if we're unaware of who we're being, what we're doing, and the impact that we're creating?

I remember later seeing that image being used on social media as a marketing tool. It didn't feel right, nor did it feel integral. First off, I never gave permission to have my photos taken that day (yes, consent is always necessary), nor did I give permission for those photos to be used for marketing purposes. Second, the entire experience surrounding the actual photo felt fake. He was obviously just thinking about himself—again, unintentionally and unconsciously. On top of this, during our time together he had multiple scheduling errors with our calls and did not deliver on many of the promises he made. The impact of this mentorship experience ran deep. But at the end of the day, I'm grateful for it because it taught me to look past the image being portrayed by someone to recognize the humanity in all of us.

This mentor has since embarked on his own journey of inner-work, and I know that by doing so, he will uncover his potency and start being a conscious and Potent Leader versus just claiming to be one.

To be a conscious leader, you must be willing to shatter the version of you that you're living in order to find the true you within. You must uncover your potency—the medicine within you that becomes activated once you begin showing up as the fullest expression of who you are.

Fuck the image. This is about having the awareness to know who you're being, what you're doing, and the impact that you're creating at all times. Your potency is the missing ingredient to conscious leadership.

Showing up as a Potent Leader is about cultivating a sense of community for your community. And that starts with you having the courage to show up as you, so they can see themselves in you.

No filters.

No masks.

No manipulation.

This is about leading with the five connectors of Potent Leadership: Authenticity, Integrity, Transparency, Embodiment, and Vulnerability.

AUTHENTICITY

What we're seeing right now is a rise in fake authenticity—leaders positioning themselves to be authentic when really they're using manipulative tactics to fulfill an egocentric goal, such as boosting their followers, subscribers, or engagement numbers. Real authenticity is about you showing up as you, and that can only happen when you do the inner-work to become brave enough to own the real you. This is about being who you are when no one's looking.

Being authentic helps you connect with your community because they'll see you as a real person, and being real creates relatability. It's much easier to connect with an authentic leader (rather than a leader who feels "too perfect") because your audience will be able to see themselves in you.

Authenticity also acts as autofiltration, which makes it easier for your aligned audience to find you, and the misaligned audience to make their exit.

INTEGRITY

Technology makes it far too easy for people to hide the truth, deliver false stories, lie, cheat, and manipulate. As such, we're seeing more and more leaders sacrificing integrity for popularity. Leaders are consciously and unconsciously throwing their morals out the door just so they can meet their bottom line, create revenue, fulfill their goals, and fill their programs and events. These tactics can work—in fact, they do, which is why they're still being used—but they do not provide lasting results. Eventually, people see through the veil and become deeply impacted by the lack of integrity.

Leading with integrity means that you're leading with moral and ethical principles—it means that you're leading with honesty, and honesty creates lasting connection.

TRANSPARENCY

As mentioned with integrity, technology makes it far too easy to hide, lie, and manipulate the truth. You can manipulate words in your captions, over-filter your photos, cut and edit your videos, and share only what you want people to see. You can grace the stage at any event, position yourself as an expert in XYZ, and share your highlight reel. You can also lead with a series of untruths, convincing yourself that it's okay to do so because soon enough, they will be the truth. An example of this is the whole "digital nomad teaching people how to be digital nomads" when in reality, they gained the income they needed to become a digital nomad from selling people on how to be a digital nomad. Pretty fucked up, don't you think?

I remember the first time I witnessed transparency in action . . . Jenn Scalia[14] (who became my first business coach shortly after this story) had the courage to share something that coaches at that time didn't dare share—her real financial numbers. I was part of her Facebook community where she shared daily advice and offered support and videos filled with amazing content. Back then, she was supporting her clients with visibility and creating steady, 10K months. And then one day, Jenn shared a post where she explained the breakdown of her income and how sometimes a 10K month actually meant that she enrolled a 10K client, but only collected a portion of that up front, meaning she didn't actually cash in five figures that month. Her transparency blew me away! No one else was sharing this truth. Yet, after she shared with us what really goes on behind the scenes (including all her investments and expenses), I realized that this must be the truth for many coaches boasting five-figure months.

Jenn's transparency helped me see just how attainable that goal was for me—she made it feel possible versus aspirational, just by giving us a peek behind the scenes. And I trusted her immediately for choosing to let us see the whole truth instead of just a series of half-truths.

Transparency creates trust, and trust creates connection.

---

14. Jenn Scalia, mindset and strategy coach, https://jennscalia.com.

EMBODIMENT

Embodiment started to come up in my own leadership after I realized that there were a lot of things I was saying but not truly practicing. We see this a lot in leadership: telling people what to do, preaching to your audience, and offering tips and guidance but not fully embodying that in your own life. It's like you're in such a rush to be seen as a leader that you're bypassing the actual work to BE a leader.

It's easy to pick up your phone and write a post, regurgitating what you just read in a book. What's tough is integrating the knowledge from the book into your own life.

It's easy to pick up a microphone and tell your audience the exact steps they need to follow to achieve their goals. What's tough is applying those steps in your own life to achieve your goals.

It's easy to record and share a video of you talking about the importance of morning routines. What's tough is maintaining that morning routine in your own life.

Embodiment alone can shift you from unconscious leadership to Potent Leadership, because it's about being the fullest expression of everything you teach, preach, share, and speak about. It's about leading by BEING your message, and this is felt by your community because you can't fake real.

VULNERABILITY

Just as we're seeing with fake authenticity, we're also seeing an influx of fake vulnerability—leaders wearing "vulnerability" as a badge to boost their numbers and their ego.

By pure definition, when we are showing up in vulnerable ways, we are opening ourselves up to the potential of being harmed, wounded, hurt, or attacked. True vulnerability is accepting that and still choosing to be vulnerable because your intention is to create connection and serve your community. Fake vulnerability is when leaders try to control the outcome of their vulnerable display to fulfill an external goal, influenced by ego. And let's just get one thing straight: You never have to start off a vulnerable share with "Vulnerable post alert!" if you're truly being vulnerable. This is about letting yourself be seen.

Think of hedgehogs . . . they have spikes on their back for defense against predators. But if you were to flip the hedgehog onto its back, you'd see their soft, spikeless belly. Being a vulnerable leader is like letting your community see your soft, spikeless belly—it's about having your defenses down so your audience has an opportunity to truly connect with you.

Why do most leaders fear vulnerability? Because it's about letting people in . . . and let's face it, many people have wounds around letting people in and are guarded because of it. It's scary to let people in. And it can be scary to let your audience see the real you if you believe that in order to be seen as a leader, you need to know it all, have it all, and be it all. Fuck that. The new paradigm of leadership is about letting your guard down and letting your community in.

The potent paradigm for leadership is one where you let people in, create connection, and build a real community around your movement. Connection creates loyalty. When you combine these five connectors of Potent Leadership, you create a powerful, concentrated medicine—your potency.

CHAPTER 29:
YOUR POTENCY, UNLEASHED

People joke around a lot about how Canadians apologize for everything. And as a Canadian, I get it . . . we do! I was that girl who would apologize to someone if they bumped into me or scared me by accident.

But what I realized is that many of us live our lives like this—constantly apologizing for who we are in unspoken ways. And it's how I used to live my life.

I used to play small due to my fear of being seen.

I used to bite my tongue due to my fear of being abandoned.

I used to wear masks, pretend, and filter myself due to my fear of being judged.

All of which are acts that had me apologizing for who I truly was when all I desired was to feel free enough to be me.

The way in which you choose to show up says a lot about how you feel about yourself. Whether you're playing small, or biting your tongue, or wearing masks, or pretending to be someone you're not, or filtering yourself . . . you're not doing these things because of them. You're doing these things because you feel wrong or bad for who you are. You're apologizing for being you.

Your purpose, your vision, your legacy? All of these are yours to fulfill. But you can't do that by apologizing for who you are. You must dig deep, face your shit, and shift how you feel about yourself. You must uncover your potency and own it. And through that ownership, you'll step into a state of unapologeticness.

Being unapologetic isn't about "not giving a fuck"—this is about knowing what to give a fuck about. For example, things that I do give a fuck about include my family, my friends, my clients, my community, my health, my well-being, my purpose, my vision, my legacy, my integrity, deforestation in the Amazon, natural health, freedom, and child trafficking. But I do not give a fuck about the haters.

Being unapologetic is about you being your potent self, fully expressed, and deeply devoted to the things you choose to devote yourself to. And in a world where many continue to apologize for who they are, your unapologetic energy will attract those who are meant to be in your life and movement, while pushing away those who aren't. This is your medicine—this is your potency, and it acts as autofiltration.

It's exhausting to engage in apologetic acts. But do you want to know what feels really fucking good? Being your unapologetic self. And the impact that follows will be experienced by you and those around you.

The most Potent Leader is the leader who is unafraid to be fully expressed.

Let me make one thing super clear . . . I did not become potent overnight. This was and still is a journey.

The more I use my voice, the more I learn about myself.

The more I learn about myself, the more I see myself.

The more I see myself, the more seen I feel by others.

The more seen I feel, the more connected I feel.

The more connected I feel, the more I express myself.

The more I express myself, the easier it becomes to show up as my fully expressed, unapologetic self.

The more I show up as my fully expressed unapologetic self, the more potent I become.

Your potency is truly a gift—a gift that you will continue to amplify your entire life. And it's a gift that will keep on giving.

If you want to feel seen, you must first see yourself.

If you want to be heard, you must first hear yourself.

If you want to feel understood, you must first understand yourself.

If you want to feel safe, you must first create that safety within yourself.

If you want to feel free, you must create a sense of freedom within yourself.

If you want to lead, you must unleash your potency.

This is the power of your medicine.

CONCLUSION:
RECLAIM YOUR POTENCY

In a world that continues to challenge our rights, our free will, and our free speech, it's become imperative that you reclaim your potency.

We are experiencing modern-day repression, with new rules, regulations, laws, guidelines, and restrictions that have been created in an attempt to control us. The internet—the space that was once revered as that space for freedom of speech—is being challenged with a shocking increase in content takedowns as an attempt to quiet the voices of many.

We are being challenged. Those who follow the rules, regulations, laws, guidelines, and restrictions are safe. And those who question what we're being challenged with are not safe, making it easy for you to want to dilute your potency even more.

But revolutions were never started by those who followed the herd, nor were they started by those who questioned nothing. Revolutions were started by those who chose to reclaim their voice, reclaim their power, and reclaim their ability to think freely.

Revolutions were started by those who chose to reclaim their potency.

And right now, you have a choice. You can choose to continue following the herd through this repression, or you can reclaim your potency and lead.

Easier said than done? Definitely. You're experiencing an internal struggle, one that runs deep into your programming. It goes against your morals and values to sit back and do nothing, and yet it also feels unsafe to speak up.

"What if I lose followers?"

"What if my family and friends disagree?"

"What if people question me?"

"What if people judge me?"

The truth is . . . you will lose followers, you will have family members and friends disagree with you, and people will question and judge you. But what would happen if you say and do nothing? How will you feel if you continue to dilute your potency and follow the herd?

There's a risk either way: either the risk of following the herd (which comes with giving up your freedom and power) or the risk of reclaiming your potency and using your power to blaze a new trail that many may not agree with or follow. The real question is, which risk feels worth it to you?

You know in your heart what it is that you want to do. Your reclamation is calling you inward, and yet, the fear of reclaiming your potency feels heavy. The world feels divided, broken, and as if people are turning against each other. The last thing you want to do is contribute to that divide, and yet, what you need to realize is that there are people who need you—people who do not have it in them to reclaim their potency—people who need leaders like you to lead them toward a new vision.

By reclaiming your potency, you will pave the way for others to do the same. This is about you demonstrating what is possible for those who want the same but believe that it isn't possible.

The revolution that is taking place in our world is one of reclamation. This is an opportunity for humanity to break the cage that has been built for us by breaking the cage that we've built around ourselves.

The freedom that you seek starts within you.

It always starts within. The moment you break the cage that you built to keep you safe will be the moment that you reclaim your potency. That potency is what will help you break the cage that has been built around you by society—the cage of rules, regulations, laws, guidelines, and restrictions that were created as an attempt to control you.

This isn't about rebellion against humanity, neither is it about the destruction of society—this is about reclamation. This is about owning your right to BE in your power, to use your voice, to think freely so that humanity can move forward together.

This is about you reclaiming your potency.

So, rise up, leader. Express yourself fully without holding anything back. Own your medicine and unapologetically share that medicine with the world.

BE the Potent Leader you know you're here to be.

ABOUT THE AUTHOR

Ruby Fremon is a certified life coach, NLP practitioner, leadership mentor, and speaker who has helped thousands gain the confidence to quit performing, crystalize their messaging, and lead their movements with integrity.

An expert on personal growth and inner-work, Ruby is the host of top-rated podcast "Potent Truth" (formerly known as "Today's Thought Leader") and has appeared in over one hundred publications and podcasts. She works with her clients one on one or in group settings at her live retreats and in her Collective.

Known for her big heart, no-bullshit approach, and shamanic gifts, Ruby's work bridges the gap between practicality and spirituality, offering leaders an opportunity to create true inner-expansion. Her favorite topics to speak on include potent leadership and conscious entrepreneurship, which have landed her on stages around the world.

Ruby sees herself as an advocate for humanity, and she uses her online presence to encourage her community to question the narrative and cultivate true sovereignty of mind, body, and spirit. She currently lives in Austin, Texas, with her husband and their two dogs, Luke and Leia. This is her first book.

LET'S DIVE DEEPER.

Now, more than ever, the world needs YOU. My hope is that this book acted as a catalyst for your potency, so you can start leading with truth, authenticity and integrity. If you're ready to deepen your inner-work and be part of a movement that will redefine leadership for humanity, I invite you to:

DOWNLOAD MY FREE GIFT TO YOU

This is a set of three activating audios to support you in diving deeper into the contents of this book.

www.potentleadership.com/gift

Or text **#GIFT** to **1-781-336-0160**
to receive the audios by phone.

JOIN THE POTENT LEADERSHIP EMAIL COMMUNITY

As you know, the digital world continues to change rapidly when it comes to social media. With a constant surge of new platforms and the demise of old platforms, I've decided to bring my community closer by offering a way for us to stay connected, despite the ongoing changes online.

www.potentleadership.com/community

Or text **#POTENTLEADERS** to **1-781-336-0160** to join.

SUBSCRIBE TO THE POTENT TRUTH PODCAST

Where today's leaders gather to question the narrative, uncover potent truth, and lead with sovereignty. I release new episodes weekly and host thought-provoking conversations with some of the world's most dynamic and disruptive leaders. Potent Truth is currently hosted on iTunes, Spotify, and all other podcast platforms, as well as on YouTube (under my channel).

www.rubyfremon.com/listen

GROW OUR MOVEMENT

Share your biggest insights, shifts, breakthroughs, and a-ha moments from the book by using the hashtag **#POTENTLEADERSHIP**. By doing so, you'll also gain a chance to be featured on my social media.

I would appreciate your feedback on what chapters helped you most, and what you would like to see in future books.

If you enjoyed this book and found it helpful, please leave a REVIEW on Amazon.

Visit us at www.potentleadership.com where you can sign up for email updates.

THANK YOU!

CPSIA information can be obtained
at www.ICGtesting.com
Printed in the USA
LVHW010737090721
692201LV00009B/580/J